Sharpe
CHEFS

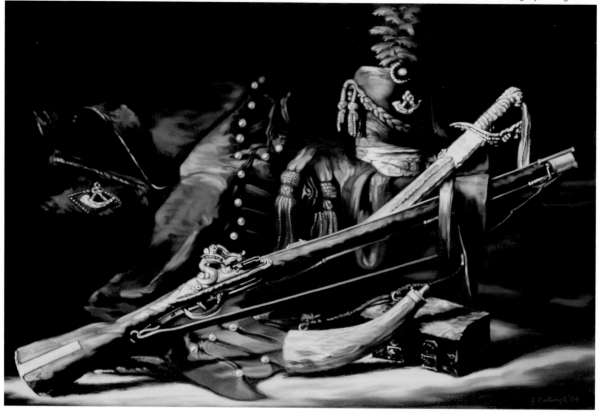

Text copyright 2007 © Adele James

Recipe photographic copyright © Individual Recipe Suppliers*

Sharpe images copyright © Picture Palace, Rex Features, Jason Salkey, Garry Cartwright

ISBN: 1-905278-16-0

Published & Printed by Pickard Communication, 11 Riverside Park, Sheaf Gardens, Sheffield S2 4BB

Telephone 0114 275 7222   Facsimile 0114 275 8866

www.pickardcommunication.co.uk

*All recipe images have been taken by the contributors themselves and not by professional photographers.

a foreword by
Bernard Cornwell

Richard Sharpe likes his food, though it is really only in *Sharpe's Enemy* that he has a chance to eat truly well. Most of the time he endures salted ration meat and twice-baked bread, a diet more or less guaranteed to shatter your teeth and ruin your digestion, but not bad if washed down with plenty of rum. In all the twenty-one (so far) Sharpe books he only, I think, cooks once, but as I included that recipe in this book I shall not repeat it here, but would recommend any adventurous cook to try it. He was very partial to the strong garlic sausages that many French soldiers carried looped from their rucksacks and, being a very English Englishman, he had a passion for roast beef.

In that he is like me. Fate (and Cupid's arrow) determined that I should live in the United States, which is made bearable by the fact that American beef can be wonderful, and that my Pennsylvania-born wife cooks a marvellous Yorkshire Pudding and that she was trained in an English pub in the proper way to roast potatoes. She perversely adds vegetables to what would otherwise be the perfect meal, and seems to think there is a virtue in salads, but in every other respect she is an amazingly wonderful cook. Too good really, because I rather enjoy cooking, but whenever Judy hears the clink of pans in the kitchen she insists on wanting to know what I'm doing and usually takes over out of exasperation with my perverse slowness. The one time I am allowed free run of the kitchen is at the beginning of November when I make a vast Christmas cake which is then fed weekly transfusions of brandy and Grand Marnier. American cakes are pathetic affairs, little more than sponges, and so I do my best to bring a little civilisation to their benighted lives. I am also allowed to make one cassoulet per winter, and as much gazpacho as I like through the summer.

Sharpe, I think, must have tasted gazpacho in his Spanish years and, even though it is composed entirely of vegetables, he probably approved of it. He would certainly have approved of this cookbook, which combines usefulness with support for a truly deserving cause. My sympathy for sufferers of osteoporosis was hugely increased this last winter when the Pennsylvania-born cook was blown by a sudden and violent gust of wind from the steps of St Paul's Cathedral in London and suffered a shattered hip. For two months the poor thing (usually a yoga teacher and fitness freak) could not move effectively and so I took over the kitchen and a succession of stews, pies and roasts was triumphantly produced, while breakfasts were proper affairs of bacon, eggs, sausages, and that great Pennsylvania delicacy, scrapple (scrapple is compressed offal and quite miraculously delicious). Judy is now recovered and salads once again appear, but so do roast beef and Yorkshire pudding, and thus peace and happiness reigns, as I trust they will reign in your house as you try the splendid recipes in this equally splendid cookbook!

Bernard Cornwell

Table of Contents

Introduction

Books are inspired in different ways. Some make a point, others impart information or permit authors to explore ideas and dreams. This project was born out of friendship.

All the Sharpe Chefs are friends, though many of us have never met in person. Our friendship grew out of a mutual admiration for the actor Sean Bean and his work; in particular, his role as the inimitable British soldier, Richard Sharpe. His acting talents are second to none, in genres that run from history to fantasy to Shakespeare. On stage, television and film, he approaches every role with depth, sympathy, passion and humour.

The Sharpe Chefs met on the internet and have all become good friends in real life. We wanted to thank Sean for being the inspiration for bringing us all together. Rather than personal thanks, hand-knitted tea cosies, or gushing fan-mail, we came upon the idea of doing something for a charity of which he is a patron - the National Osteoporosis Society (NOS) (plus osteoporosis is a condition that affects one in two women and we are all women).

A cookery book seemed a logical choice and one in which we could share our international cooking traditions.

We asked Mr. Cornwell if he would consent to our use of Sharpe-related names in the book. He agreed straight away. In fact, he has written our foreword and donated two recipes from Richard Sharpe himself! Added to this we were sent recipes from many other Chosen Men!

This not just a cookery book.

- The National Osteoporosis Society has kindly donated a piece about osteoporosis, and there are many additional facts about osteoporosis
- There are historical notes (and recipes)
- There is a piece about cauldron cooking, a method of cooking commonly used during the Peninsular Wars, and another about the type of food a young Richard Sharpe might have encountered in England
- Above all, there is an abundance of love and affection poured into these pages from the combined hearts of a group of women who can call each other friends

From all of us, a big Thank You for buying this book and supporting the National Osteoporosis Society.

The Sharpe Chefs

For **Sean Bean**
- who inspired our friendships.

ACKNOWLEDGEMENTS

The Sharpe Chefs would like to offer our grateful thanks to the following people:

To Bernard Cornwell
for all his help and support, given so generously
(and for writing the Sharpe books in the first place!).

To Cece who has always looked out for us.

To Chris at the Sharpe Appreciation Society - www.southessex.co.uk
who helped us contact The Chosen Men.

To Pauline Climpson for all her help.

To Dave Harris at Low Light Images - www.lowlightimages.com

To Muzzick for sharing her cyber home with us.

To Paul Reynolds who led us to our publisher.

To the Chosen Men (and Women)
Jason Salkey, Daragh O'Malley, Lyndon Davies, Michael Mears,
Paul and Penny Trussell and John and Sally Tams for their recipes.

To Tom Clegg, Muir Sutherland and Malcolm Craddock for their recipes.

To Malcolm Craddock at Picture Palace for kindly letting us use Sharpe photographs.

To Jason Salkey for kindly supplying photographs from his collection - www.riflemanharris.co.uk

To Rex Features for kindly allowing us to use their Sharpe photographs.

To Garry Cartwright for kindly letting us reproduce his Sharpe paintings.

To Gary Mackender for his wonderful design work
(of course being a Sharpe fan helped!!)

To Mick Liversidge and Chris Pickard at Pickard Communication,
for having faith in our project and making the dream come true.

To our families who have supported us while we worked on this labour of love.

Sean Bean

As a patron of the National Osteoporosis Society, I am delighted to put my name to this book.

Osteoporosis is a disease that affects so many men and women and the NOS helps both them and their families to cope.

By being a part of the Sharpe Chefs, I am able to further support the NOS and their work.

I hope you enjoy the book and while you are trying some recipes, you will know that you have helped give something towards a very worthwhile charity.

Osteoporosis - **The Silent Disease**

The National Osteoporosis Society is the only national charity dedicated to improving the prevention, diagnosis, and treatment of this fragile bone disease.

The bones in our skeleton are made of a thick outer shell and a strong inner mesh which looks like honeycomb made up of bony struts. Osteoporosis means some of these struts become thin or break, making the bone more fragile and prone to fracture. Osteoporosis is called the silent disease because it often remains undetected until the time of the first broken bone, which can occur in the wrist, hip or spine. Bone loss occurs naturally in everyone as they get older but these broken bones are not an inevitable part of ageing and there is much that can be done to prevent and treat them.

In the UK, one in two women and one in five men over the age of 50 will break a bone, mainly because of osteoporosis, although it can affect people of all ages. Three million people are at risk of osteoporosis in the UK, but this risk can be reduced by taking plenty of weight bearing exercise and eating healthily throughout life.

Men and women are at increased risk if they:

- Have a low body weight (women who are under weight or have developed an eating disorder)
- Drink excessive amounts of alcohol or smoke heavily
- Take high doses of corticosteroid tablets (taken for conditions such as asthma and arthritis)
- Live with medical conditions which leave them immobile for a long time
- Have a family history of osteoporosis, particularly if their mother has broken her hip
- Have a medical condition which affects the absorption of foods, such as Crohn's disease and coeliac disease

Men with low levels of the male hormone testosterone, a condition called hypogonadism, are at a higher risk of osteoporosis, while women with a lack of oestrogen caused by early menopause (before the age of 45) or early hysterectomy (before the age of 45), especially if both ovaries are removed, are at a higher risk. Another risk factor for women is missing periods for six months or more (excluding pregnancy) as a result of over-exercising or over-dieting.

If you think you are at risk then you need to discuss it further with your GP. The GP will assess your medical history, including whether you have broken any bones or lost height, and may decide to send you for a special scan to measure your bone density. The Dual Energy X-ray Absorptiometry (DXA) scans and measures the density of bones. This test is currently the most accurate and reliable way to find out the strength of bones and your risk of breaking a bone. It is a simple, painless procedure that uses very low doses of radiation. You will be asked to lie down for 10-15 minutes while an x-ray arm passes over you to take an image of your hip or spine. These scanners are usually in hospitals and not all hospitals have one, which can mean long waiting times.

If you have already broken a bone after a minor bump or fall you may already have osteoporosis. Other warning signs include height loss and kyphosis (curvature of the spine). We cannot see or feel our bones becoming more fragile as we get older so we can be quite unaware of any problems with our skeleton.

If you have osteoporosis, your GP may prescribe a drug treatment to help treat the disease. Some of these drugs work by slowing down the activity of demolition cells while others stimulate the construction cells to build more bone. Some drugs work on both sets of cells. If you do not have osteoporosis, there is a lot you can do to try to build and maintain a strong skeleton that will help to prevent osteoporosis.

It is essential to try to eat well-balanced, calcium-rich food throughout life to give you all the vitamins and minerals you need to help develop and maintain strong, healthy bones. Aim to eat meals that incorporate foods from the four main groups, including fruit and vegetables; carbohydrates like bread, potatoes, pasta and cereals; milk and dairy products; and proteins such as meat, fish, eggs, pulses and nuts.

Calcium is the most abundant mineral found in bones and helps to give them strength and rigidity. Excellent sources of calcium are milk and dairy products, including the low fat varieties. You can also find calcium in a wide range of other foods such as green leafy vegetables, dried fruit, tinned fish (provided you eat the bones) and tofu (a type of vegetable protein made from soya beans). Adults should aim to eat 700mg of calcium every day.

You also need vitamin D to help your body absorb calcium. The best source is sunlight. About 15 – 20 minutes of sun exposure to the face and arms every day during the summer should provide you with enough vitamin D throughout the year, but be careful not to allow your skin to burn.

Bone is a living tissue and needs to be exercised just like muscles. Your skeleton grows stronger if you do weight-bearing exercise. This is any kind of physical activity where you are supporting the weight of your own body such as jogging, aerobics, tennis, dancing and even brisk walking. Try to exercise at least three times a week for a minimum of twenty minutes.

You can also help your bones by giving up smoking and watching how much alcohol you drink. You should aim not to exceed the government's recommended limit. It is always good to have alcohol-free days. Men should drink no more than 21 units of alcohol per week (and no more than four units in any one day) and women should drink no more than 14 units of alcohol per week (and no more than three units in any one day). If you are pregnant, the government advises that you do not drink at all.

For more information visit the National Osteoporosis Society website at **www.nos.org.uk** or call their helpline at **0845 450 0230** (9am – 5pm Monday to Friday).

Conversion Tables

LIQUID MEASURE CONVERSIONS

5ml	= 1 teaspoon	
10ml	= 1 dessertspoon	= 2 teaspoons
15ml	= 3 teaspoons	= 1 tablespoon = $\frac{1}{2}$ fl.oz
30ml	= 2 tablespoons	= 1 tablespoon = 1 fl.oz

Metric	Imperial oz	US Cups	US Pints
30ml	1 fl.oz	$\frac{1}{8}$	
60ml	2 fl.oz	$\frac{1}{4}$	
120ml	4 fl.oz	$\frac{1}{2}$	$\frac{1}{4}$ pt
150ml	5 fl.oz		$\frac{1}{4}$ pt
180ml	6 fl.oz	$\frac{3}{4}$	
240ml	8 fl.oz	1	$\frac{1}{2}$pt
300ml	10 fl.oz	$1\frac{1}{4}$	$\frac{1}{2}$pt
360ml	12 fl.oz	$1\frac{1}{2}$	$\frac{3}{4}$pt
420ml	14 fl.oz	$1\frac{3}{4}$	
480ml	16 fl.oz	2	1pt
600ml	20 fl.oz	$2\frac{1}{2}$	1pt
960ml	32 fl.oz	4	1 quart
1.1L	40 fl.oz	5	$2\frac{1}{2}$pts

WEIGHT CONVERSION

Metric	Imperial
25g	1oz
50g	2oz
100g	4oz = $\frac{1}{4}$lb
225g	8oz = $\frac{1}{2}$lb
325g	12oz = $\frac{3}{4}$lb
350g	13oz
450g	16oz = 1lb
675g	22oz = $1\frac{1}{2}$lb
1kg	2.2lb
1.2kg	$2\frac{1}{2}$lb
1.3kg	3lb
1.8kg	4lb
2.2kg	5lb

OVEN TEMPERATURE CONVERSIONS

Centigrade	Fahrenheit	Gas Mark	Heat
110	225	$\frac{1}{4}$	Very cool
130	250	$\frac{1}{2}$	
140	275	1	Cool
150	300	2	
170	325	3	Moderate
180	350	4	
190	375	5	Moderately hot
200	400	6	
220	425	7	Hot
230	450	8	
240	475	9	Very hot

www.riflemanharris.co.uk

Sharpe's Recipes

Sharpe's Recipes

Special contributions from the people who know Sharpe best!

The editors are extremely grateful to Mr. Bernard Cornwell for sharing his thoughts and these recipes from Richard Sharpe!

"Richard Sharpe was never really noted for his cooking, though he certainly appreciated good food and was always happy to roast, fry, skewer or broil frogs. Still, as he's been asked to provide two recipes for this cookbook, here they are. One is all his own, the other he stole from Lucille, the woman with whom he lived so happily when the wars were at last all over. Lucille, of course, is French, and though her recipe is very simple, it is also delicious."

LUCILLE'S LEG OF LAMB

You're going to need:
a half leg of lamb;
use the shank/knuckle end
1 tablespoon of olive oil
3 to 4 sprigs of fresh thyme
one glass of white wine
salt

This is a really delicious way to serve lamb, it's very simple to prepare, but it does take a long time to cook!
That's the point, that the cooking is really slow . . .

Brown the leg gently in the olive oil.
Use a heavy casserole pan. When the leg is browned (i.e. sealed) add all the other ingredients and put in a medium oven (Gas Mark 4) for at least 3 hours! At least! 4 hours is fine. That's it! Serve with whatever; new potatoes and peas are nice.

SHARPE'S LEG OF CHEVAL

You're going to need:
1 sword or bayonet
1 dead French cavalry horse
axle grease from a field gun
camp fire
breastplate from a captured
French cuirassier

I think this is the only meal Sharpe cooks in the series, and he and Harper ate it with evident enjoyment, so you might like it too.

Find your horse. Cut fresh large chunk of meat from rump with sword or bayonet. Build a fire. Put the breastplate on the fire. Slap in axle grease you scooped from gun. Fry meat in axle grease. Eat. Then realise how grateful Sharpe was to meet Lucille.

Bernard Cornwell

Bernard Cornwell was born in London in 1944 - a 'warbaby' - whose father was a Canadian airman and mother in Britain's Women's Auxiliary Air Force. Adopted by a family in Essex who belonged to a religious sect called the Peculiar People (and they were), he escaped to London University and, after a stint as a teacher, joined BBC Television where he worked for the next 10 years. While working as Head of Current Affairs Television for the BBC in Northern Ireland, he met Judy, a visiting American, and fell in love. Judy was unable to move to Britain for family reasons so Bernard went to the States where he was refused a Green Card. He decided to earn a living by writing, a job that did not need a permit from the US government - and for some years he had been wanting to write the adventures of a British soldier in the Napoleonic wars - and so the Sharpe series was born. Bernard and Judy married in 1980, are still married, still live in the States and he is still writing Sharpe. He says, "I never thought there would be this many books - I imagined there might be ten or eleven - but then along came Sean Bean and the television programmes and I virtually began a whole new Sharpe series."

To find out more, visit **www.bernardcornwell.net**

The Sharpe Series to date:

Sharpe's Tiger (1799)
Richard Sharpe and the Siege of Seringapatam

Sharpe's Triumph (September 1803)
Richard Sharpe and the Battle of Assaye

Sharpe's Fortress (December 1803)
Richard Sharpe and the Siege of Gawilghur

Sharpe's Trafalgar (21 October, 1805)
Richard Sharpe and the Battle of Trafalgar

Sharpe's Prey (1807)
Richard Sharpe and the Expedition to Copenhagen

Sharpe's Rifles (January 1809)
Richard Sharpe and the French Invasion of Galicia

Sharpe's Havoc (Spring 1809)
Richard Sharpe and the Campaign in Northern Portugal

Sharpe's Eagle (July 1809)
Richard Sharpe and Talavera Campaign

Sharpe's Gold (August 1810)
Richard Sharpe and the Destruction of Almeida

Sharpe's Escape (1810)
Richard Sharpe and the Bussaco Campaign

Sharpe's Fury (March 1811)
Richard Sharpe and the Battle of Barrosa

Sharpe's Battle (May 1811)
Richard Sharpe and the Battle of Fuentes de Onaro

Sharpe's Company (January to April 1812)
Richard Sharpe and the Siege of Badajoz

Sharpe's Sword (June and July 1812)
Richard Sharpe and the Salamanca Campaign

Sharpe's Enemy (Christmas 1812)
Richard Sharpe and the Defense of Portugal

Sharpe's Honour (February to June 1813)
Richard Sharpe and the Vitoria Campaign

Sharpe's Regiment (June to November 1813)
Richard Sharpe and the Invasion of France

Sharpe's Siege (1814)
Richard Sharpe and the Winter Campaign

Sharpe's Revenge (1814)
Richard Sharpe and the Peace of 1814

Sharpe's Waterloo (15 June to 18 June 1815)
Richard Sharpe and the Waterloo Campaign

Sharpe's Devil (1820-21)
Richard Sharpe and the Emperor

Sharpe's Christmas: Two short stories by Bernard Cornwell
Sharpe's Skirmish: A short story by Bernard Cornwell

Jason Salkey

WELSH RAREBIT

You're going to need:
Sharp(e) Cheddar cheese
orange cheese
mango chutney
mayonnaise

Taught to me by Sharpe caterers Rachel Browne and Giles Ashton.

Grate your cheeses (equal amounts, as much as you like). Add to a bowl.

Mix 1 or 2 teaspoons of chutney (depending on your taste and amount of cheese) in to cheese. Add enough mayonnaise to the mixture until you have a thick (not too soggy) paste.

The Diaries of Rifleman Harris

Behind the scenes of Sharpe - a unique and intimate series of films shot and composed by Jason Salkey.

To order - or find out more visit Jason's website at
www.riflemanharris.co.uk

Lightly toast some bread. Spread cheese mix evenly across toast. Place under a medium grill until cheese has started to melt. Serve with cucumbers and cherry tomatoes.

"No Name Harris"

John & Sally Tams

DARK CHOCOLATE PIE

To serve 6 you will need:
100g (3½ oz) dark chocolate
(75% cocoa solids is best)
40g (3 tbsp) unsalted butter
150ml (5oz) single cream *(I use low fat)*
2 beaten eggs
15g (1 tbsp) cocoa powder dissolved
in 5ml (1tsp) boiling water
(you might need slightly more)
55g (4½ tbsp) caster sugar
an 8 inch sweet pastry case
*(I do sometimes cheat and buy
a ready made one)*

Serve with: pouring cream and
icing sugar mixed with cocoa for dusting

Preheat oven to 180°C/Gas Mark 4/350°F.

Melt the butter and chocolate together in a pan over boiling water.

When melted, allow it to cool and then just whisk in the other ingredients.
Pour this mixture into the pastry case, place in the oven and bake for about 20 to 25 minutes.

It is delicious served hot or cold, with pouring cream and dusted with some of the icing sugar/cocoa mix.

It is also lovely served with some strawberries ......mmmmmmm

To make 34 you will need:

454g (1lb) self raising flour
(I sometimes mix wholemeal with white)
5g (1 tsp) salt
5g (1 tsp) mustard powder
2.5g (½ tsp) cayenne pepper (maximum)
114g (4oz) margarine
227g (8oz) cheese
(Red Leicester works well)
114 to 142ml (8 to 10 tbsp) milk
(I use skimmed)
5 to 10g (1-2 tsp) baking powder

A Life of Song

Although many Sharpe fans know him best as the 95th Rifles' best shot and balladeer, Rifleman Hagman, John Tams had established himself as a successful musician, songwriter, and musical director long before he took on the role.

Find out more about John's life and music at **www.johntams.co.uk**

SALLY'S MUM'S BRILLIANT CHEESE SCONES

My mum has baked this recipe for decades and still makes a batch for us when we are touring. It is the food that keeps us going at two in the morning on a long journey after a gig. Delicious with butter but less dangerous to the waistline eaten on their own! The recipe gives quantities for making 34 small scones. They freeze really well.

Heat oven to 200°C/Gas Mark 6/400°F

Rub the margarine into the flour. Add all the other dry ingredients except the cheese. Mix thoroughly. Add the cheese. Now gradually add the milk. Roll out very roughly and cut out using a small cutter (use a big cutter if you're feeling hungry or are a size zero!)

Place in the oven and bake for 12 to 15 minutes or until they are risen and golden brown. Resist eating for as long as possible - around 3 minutes is the norm!

SIMFEROPOL SAVIOUR

When John and the rest of the crew and cast were working in the Ukraine, I sent out food parcels twice a week. It was a curious mix of things that I could send, rather like a very poor bag of goods on *Ready, Steady, Cook*. Dried mash potato, Cup a Soups, tea bags, squirty cheese, tinned tuna and chocolate seemed to help.

HAGMAN'S HASH

One thing I know John used to make for the team was mashed potato, reconstituted using Cup a Soup and mixed with tinned tuna. This was served on crispbreads and accompanied with local sherry. The sheer glamour. It might sound awful - it was - but it kept them going on the days when there was no food.

Daragh O'Malley

To serve 4 you will need:

For One Step Shortcrust Pastry:
100g (4oz) soft tub margarine
175g (6oz) plain flour (sifted)
15 ml (1 tbsp) chilled water
pinch of salt

907g (2 lb) rump steak - cubed
57g (4 tbsp) plain flour
salt and pepper to taste
14g (1 tbsp) brown sugar
4 onions - chopped
400ml (13½oz) Guinness
42g (3 tbsp) raisins *(optional)*
8 slices of bacon
- chopped into bite size pieces
85g (3oz) lard
(or 28g (2 tbsp) vegetable oil)
fresh parsley - chopped

STEAK AND GUINNESS PIE

Heat oven to 180°C/Gas Mark 4/350°F

Place the margarine, 2 tablespoons of the flour and the water in a bowl. Cream with a fork for about 30 seconds until well mixed. Add the remaining flour with the salt to make a fairly soft dough and knead gently until smooth. Do not overwork the dough.

Roll out about two thirds of the dough and place into required pie dish for the base of the pie. Roll out the rest of the dough to a circle slightly larger than the size of the pie dish. Keep this for the lid.

Mix the flour, salt and pepper to taste. Cut the steak into bite-size portions and coat in the flour mixture. Put the bacon into a heavy frying pan and cook over medium heat until there is enough bacon fat to brown the beef. Remove the bacon pieces and fry the beef on medium heat until it is browned all over. With a slotted spoon, remove meat from the pan, keeping the remaining juices. Set the meat aside to cool.

Put the brown sugar, raisins and Guinness in a jug and leave until the raisins have taken in some of the liquid (about 5 minutes). If not using the raisins, simply add the sugar to the Guinness.

Cook the onions in the meat juices, adding the lard (or vegetable oil). Sauté until they turn golden. Combine the steak, onions, Guinness, and raisins (if used), in a casserole dish with a tight-fitting lid; cook for 2½ hours. Stir occasionally, adding more beer if the rich brown gravy appears too thick. After 2½ hours, remove from oven and take off the lid.

Turn the oven to 190°C/Gas Mark 5/375°F. Prick the pastry lining in the pie dish with a floured fork and cook until browned (around 8 to 10 minutes depending on your oven). Remove from oven. Pour the steak mixture into the cooked pie base. Place the dough lid on the top and pinch the edges together all around. Use a fork to pierce the top for steam holes. Return to the oven for 10 minutes. Remove and allow to cool for 10 minutes before serving.

Paul Trussell

To serve 6 you will need:

12 sausages
(well-flavoured ones like
Toulouse are good)
oil
1 large onion, in large dice
1 large leek, in large rings
3 carrots, in large slices
2 medium courgettes, in large slices
10 mushrooms, halved
2 cloves garlic, chopped finely
2 tins of tomatoes, chopped
1.5 pints chicken stock
large handful pot barley
red wine
tomato purée
bouquet garni
1 teaspoon sugar
salt and pepper
large, heavy based, hob & ovenproof
casserole pan, with a lid

ISAIAH'S TONGUE TICKLING SAUSAGE CASSEROLE
By Paul and Penny Trussell

Heat oven to 160°C/Gas Mark 4/350°F

Chop up each sausage into four stumpy cylinders. Heat a tablespoonful of oil in the casserole pan. Add sausage chunks, in a single layer, so as not to overcrowd the pan, and fry over a high heat until well-browned. You will probably have to do this in two or more batches – so between batches remove the browned sausages with a slotted spoon, and keep to one side.

When all sausage chunks are browned, remove the last batch from the pan and keep with the others. The sausages will have begun to give up their fat; now use this to fry the vegetables, adding a little more oil if necessary. Turn the heat down to medium, add the onion and cook until golden brown and softened. Add the carrot and fry (with the lid on to create some steam), for around 5 minutes until beginning to soften. Add the leek, courgette and garlic and cook for a further 5 minutes, stirring occasionally.

Deglaze the pan with a good glug of red wine, then return the sausage chunks to the pan. Add the tinned tomatoes, 2 tablespoons of tomato purée, the stock, bouquet garni, sugar, ground black pepper, and the barley. Stir everything together, cover with the lid, and put it in the oven for around an hour and a half, until the barley is plump and the casserole is looking thick and rich. Season to taste. Put the mushrooms into the pan for the final 10 minutes of cooking (unless you're making it in advance, in which case, see below). You will need to stir the casserole a few times during its oven cooking. (If you prefer, you could simmer the casserole on the hob over a low heat for an hour and a half, instead of in the oven.)

This casserole benefits from being cooked some time in advance of eating so it's good to serve if you're cooking for friends, or if you want to make a batch in advance to freeze or eat later in the week. The flavours blend and mellow really nicely upon reheating. Simply heat it through on the hob or in the oven again when you want to eat it. In this case, don't put the mushrooms in until you reheat; then just add them in for 10 minutes or so to cook through.

To serve, try it with brown rice and maybe some steamed green beans or mangetout, or even just some crusty bread. You can vary the vegetables in the casserole depending on what you have, or what's in season.

Michael Mears

To serve 2 you will need:
113g (¹/₄ lb) liver (calf, lamb, or ox)
227g (¹/₂ lb) onions
salt and pepper
oil

Slice the onions as thinly as possible *(a mandolin works well for this)*. Coat the bottom of a heavy frying pan with oil; add the onions and season with salt and pepper. Cover and cook over very low heat for 30 to 40 minutes. Do not allow the onions to burn!

Using an extremely sharp knife, slice the liver as thinly as possible; this is a slightly easier task if you chill the liver until it is almost frozen. Add the liver to the pan with the cooked onions and continue cooking until the liver is done.

FEGATO ALLA VENEZIANA, OR LIVER VENETIAN STYLE

They say every man can cook one dish, if nothing else, and I'm no exception. That dish is usually spag bol, and I certainly do rustle up a nice version of that (well, I am half-Italian after all!). But I have a second dish up my sleeve - far fewer men can say that, I believe. It's a real pauper's meal, from my student days - well, it's good for students and soldiers too! In fact, it's a cheap, simple, but very tasty dish and perfect to warm you up on a cold winter's night. Once again, there is an Italian influence, as the dish is Fegato alla Veneziana, or Liver Venetian style. I know it's the kind of thing Rifleman Cooper would enjoy, because, well, let him take over . . .

Yeh, when you get down to it, it's the kind of grub I like to eat down in Shoreditch, it's really just liver and onions, ain't it? Difference is, what you do with the onions, that's what makes it Italian, I suppose. I dunno. What I do know is it's damn tasty.

To cook enough for you and your lady-friend (if you're a bloke - or for your Rifleman if you're a lady), get a quarter pound of liver (calves or lambs is best, but ox liver will serve), half a pound of onions from Shoreditch market, or wherever you live will do, and the only other things you need are salt, pepper and oil - and an APPETITE of course!

Now, slice the onions really finely, and I mean, FINELY. Get yourself a heavy frying pan, cover it with a thin layer of oil, then shove the onions in, with some salt and pepper, and cook 'em gently, and I mean gently, for 30-40 minutes. Bung a cover on top while they're cooking, or stewing rather. This is the Italian bit you see. Those onions will be so sweet and tender. Don't let 'em burn, I'm warning you!

In the meantime get your sharpest knife out (a bayonet will serve) and shave the thinnest possible slices off your liver (well, not YOUR liver, the liver you've bought for cooking.) If it's calves' liver it'll only need 2 or 3 minutes cooking with the onions. If it's lamb's or ox liver, you'll have to add it to the onions after half an hour and then cook it for another quarter hour.

You can serve this up just as it is, or bung it on top of some plain boiled rice. Or have it with some spuds and cabbage. I'm telling you, it's simple and it's tasty and it'll keep you lovely and warm on those dark winter nights. Cooper's verdict: NICE!

Oh, but not for vegetarians, I suppose. Sorry.

Lyndon Davies

To serve 4 you will need:

1 large sweet potato,
peeled and cut into chunks

4 large carrots *(or 8 small)*,
peeled and chopped

2 medium red onions,
roughly chopped up

1-2 red chilli's

2-3 cloves of garlic

20g (1½ tbsp) butter

1L (4 cups) vegetable stock

pepper to taste

SWEET PERKINS' SOUP

I thought I would try you with a favourite soup of mine (actually I stole the recipe from my girlfriend). I love it for its great taste and simplicity; I hope you enjoy it too.

Melt the butter in a large saucepan, then add all the vegetables, chilli and garlic. Stir on a low heat for 10-15 minutes. Add the stock and boil until all the veg has softened. Leave it to cool before blending and reheating. Delicious on its own or garnished with some chunks of goat's cheese and pepper to taste.

"Any Rifleman who puts four shots into the round target, or three in the body of the man in the canvas one, out of six...for two days practice out of three...will be ranked in the class of marksman, and wear the green cockade. Any Rifleman who puts in two shots in the round target, or two in the body of the man, at the 2nd range and upwards, out of six, for two days firing out of three...(will) wear the small white cockade".

Tom Clegg

To serve 4 you will need:
680g (1½ lbs) scrag end of mutton
2 sheep's kidneys
1 onion
907g (2 lbs) potatoes
pepper and salt
237ml (½ pint) water
dripping or butter

LANCASHIRE HOT POT

Heat oven to 180°C/Gas Mark 4/350°F

Grease an oven-proof dish and put in a thick layer of sliced potato. Cut the meat into small to medium pieces and place on top of the potatoes. Cover with sliced onion and salt and pepper to taste. Pour on the water. Place the remaining potato slices, cut in halves, to cover the meat. Brush over the potatoes with a little melted fat/butter.

Cook for about 2 hours.

Muir Sutherland

Mercedes' Recipes!

You're going to need:
4 medium size eggs
200g (7oz) white sugar
200g (7oz) ground almonds
the grated rind of 1 lemon

TARTA DE SANTIAGO

Whisk eggs and sugar together adding the lemon rind.
When beaten add ground almonds slowly then beat the mixture.

Prepare medium size cooking tin with melted butter in bottom of tin.
Put all elements in cooking tin then cook 20/30 minutes at 190 degrees.

You're going to need:
5 medium size potatoes
1 large Spanish onion
4/5 eggs

SPANISH OMELETTE

Peel potatoes and onion then cut into small pieces.

Prepare a pan with olive oil. When hot fry potatoes and onion.
When mixture is cooked whisk eggs adding salt and pepper.
Strain oil from potatoes and onion, leave for ten minutes then mix with eggs and add to pan.

Using a plate turn the pan over twice.

Serve with mixed salad (olives/tomatoes/lettuce/chicory).

Malcolm Craddock

CHICKEN AND APRICOTS IN ARMAGNAC

You're going to need:

1 oven-ready capon 10-12 lb

seasoning

a little red wine for gravy

FOR THE APRICOTS IN ARMAGNAC

325g (12oz) dried, stoned apricots

600ml (20 fl oz) cold, Earl Grey tea

50g (2oz) granulated sugar

150ml (5 fl oz) Armagnac

FOR THE APPLE STUFFING

675g (1 1/2 lb) Bramley apples, cut into half inch slices

225g (1/2 lb) dried, stoned apricots, chopped

1 large onion, chopped

30 ml (2 tbsp) Armagnac

small pinch ground cloves

pinch ground mace

salt

FOR THE FORCEMEAT STUFFING

capon liver, chopped

1 Cox's apple, chopped

1 medium onion

50g (2oz) breadcrumbs

10g (2 tsp) dried sage

seasoning

My wife Rachel is always complaining that I can't cook, even when I tell her that I once cooked Capon in Armagnac for 4 people one Christmas lunch - several years before I met Rachel of course. It was a very nerve wracking experience, but as I was able to follow a recipe, it all ended in success, although I did have to call on Toby Eady a couple of times for advice on how long to cook the capon and followed his advice. Here is the recipe for my famous Christmas dish.

Preheat oven to 160-170°C/Gas Mark 3-4/325°F

Soak apricots overnight in the cold tea, drain and barely cover with water, add sugar and simmer for 15 minutes. Drain, sprinkle with the Armagnac, cover and leave in the fridge.

Mix all the apple stuffing ingredients together and, separately, mix all the forcemeat stuffing ingredients together. Place the forcemeat stuffing into the neck flap end of the bird, pressing it in as far as you can, tucking the neck flap all round, then secure the flap underneath with a small skewer. Place the apple stuffing in the body cavity.

Season the capon to taste, lay on a rack in a roasting tin, then place in the centre of the pre-heated oven. Roast for 30 minutes to the pound plus 45 minutes.

The capon is cooked when juices run clear when you pierce the thickest part of the leg. Remove to serving dish, snap off wing tips and rest for 20 minutes.

Drain the fat from the tin and make gravy from residue, plus giblet stock and wine. Heat the apricots gently and serve.

Starters & Appetisers

Starters & Appetisers

Appetisers? Sharpe's men would have been amazed to think that people needed these.
To them, an appetiser was a lump of stale bread they chewed while hungrily waiting for the meat in the
cauldron to be rendered edible. Somehow, all that hard marching and inflicting serious damage on the
French whetted their appetites beyond the point of needing assistance!

Things were different in the more rarefied confines of the Officers Mess, especially on 'Ladies' Night'.
No doubt, delicate morsels were produced to sharpen the enjoyment of a good meal. The officers had
certain benefits denied to Sharpe's men, such as extra provisions and skilled cooks. Although it feels a
little disloyal to those brave enlisted soldiers, we recommend that you emulate the officers and make full
use of the dishes described in this section. Unless, of course, you have been marching and inflicting
serious damage on an enemy, in which case, feel free to make use of the stale bread hint!

Lord Wellington's Crab Dip

To serve 10

Preheat oven to 180°C/Gas Mark 4/350°F

Combine, mixing thoroughly:

680g (24oz) cream cheese, softened

89ml (6 tbsp) whole milk

45ml (3 tbsp) Worcestershire sauce

10 drops hot sauce (Tabasco)

184g (6 1/2 oz) crab meat, canned

Put in an oven proof dish and bake 30 to 35 minutes.

Serve warm with dipping crisps or crackers.

Ross's Spinach, Broccoli & Artichoke Dip

Though General Ross would announce his presence on the field of battle with the skirl of bagpipes, you won't have to pipe this calcium and vitamin rich dip into the room to impress family and friends alike! Make it ahead without the Cheddar on top and keep it in the refrigerator for up to 2 days. Take it out, heat it up, top with Cheddar and heat again to melt the cheese. Vary the garlic to suit your taste.

Mix:

567g (2½ cups) frozen chopped spinach, thawed
284g (1¼ cup) frozen chopped broccoli, thawed

Sauté in olive oil:

1 large onion, chopped
2 to 5 garlic cloves, chopped
add the spinach/broccoli mixture, add a bit more oil; sauté until tender and then add salt to taste and:
170 – 227g (6 – 8oz) marinated artichokes, tinned or jarred
Sauté 5 minutes more and then add:
227g (8oz) room temperature cream cheese

Stir until the cheese melts and add 170g (6oz) flaked almonds. Add hot sauce (Tabasco) to taste (3 to 12 drops). Spray a microwave dish with cooking spray and add the mix to the dish. Cover with grated Cheddar cheese (about 170g).

Place in microwave or oven to melt the cheese; this dish is best served hot.

To make a spicier version add 16g (4tsp) dried red pepper flakes along with the hot sauce.

Hagman's Cheese & Garlic Dip

Combine in a food processor until thoroughly mixed and then chill until serving time:

113g (4oz) room temperature cream cheese
170g (6oz) crumbled Feta or Blue cheese
80–160ml (1/3 to 2/3 cup) mayonnaise
2 cloves garlic, minced
2g (½ tsp) dried basil
2g (½ tsp) dried oregano
2g (½ tsp) dried dill

Garrard's Cheese & Sherry Spread

"Eh, Tom, glad to see ya survived the explosion."
"No thanks to you, Dick - we barely made it out alive.
I just managed to nick this bottle of sherry before the fort went off."
"Well, I've a bit of curry here and the lads have some cheese - think we could come up with a bit of dinner?"

Combine, mixing thoroughly:
170g (6oz) cream cheese, softened
140g (5oz) mature Cheddar cheese, grated
75ml (5 tbsp) dry sherry
5g (1 tsp) curry powder
5g (1 tsp) salt

Spread the mixture about 2.5cm (1 inch) thick on a serving plate and chill until firm.

Before serving, remove from refrigerator and spread on top:

240g (8^{1}/$_{2}$ oz) chutney
6 finely chopped green onions (scallions)

Let the spread reach room temperature before serving. This can be made 2 to 3 days ahead of time but do not top until serving day.

Recruiters during the Peninsular War relied on a variety of means to acquire volunteers for the army. Paltry military pay and severe discipline did little to tempt any but the most desperate men; recruiters were infamous for plying potential recruits with liquor to accept the King's shilling. Criminals facing transportation, men who sought to avoid arrest for abandoning their wives and children to the care of local parishes, orphans, and boys from workhouses were also favourite targets of sergeants trying to earn their own shillings by enlisting recruits. The troops that resulted from these tactics were not always dedicated soldiers – at the battle of Waterloo, the Duke of Wellington called his men "the scum of the earth."

Beer-Battered Asparagus Poppers

To serve 4 you will need:
For dipping sauce:
120ml (1/2 cup) mayonnaise
15ml (1 tbsp) Dijon mustard
1g (1/4 tsp) black pepper
stir together mayonnaise, mustard, and pepper in a small bowl. Chill, covered

For asparagus:
227g (1 cup) plain flour
5g (1 tsp) salt
237ml (1 cup) Guinness
(do not measure foam)
900g (2 lbs) small asparagus, trimmed and cut into 3-inch pieces
about 950ml (4 cups) vegetable oil

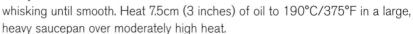

Preheat oven to very low (93°C/Gas Mark 1/4 /200°F)

Whisk together flour and salt in a bowl until combined, then slowly add beer, whisking until smooth. Heat 7.5cm (3 inches) of oil to 190°C/375°F in a large, heavy saucepan over moderately high heat.

Submerge asparagus pieces in batter to coat. Working in batches of 10, add the pieces to the oil one at a time, first gently shaking to remove excess batter. Stir gently to keep asparagus from sticking together. Fry until golden, 2 to 3 minutes. Transfer with a slotted spoon to a paper-towel-lined baking sheet and keep warm in oven. Return oil to 190°C between batches.

Keep warm in oven no more than 30 minutes; serve with Dijon Sauce.

Helena's (The Marquesa) Cheese & Olive Bites

Preheat oven to 175°C/Gas Mark 4 /350°F
You will need: the required number of stuffed olives
Mix:
113g (1/2 cup) butter, softened
227g (1 cup) plain flour
227g (8oz) mature Cheddar cheese, grated

Roll a small amount of this mixture around well-drained, stuffed olives. The size of the olives determines the number of servings you can make. Bake for 15 to 18 minutes or until light brown. Remove from oven and serve warm. These can be made ahead, refrigerated and baked just before you serve them.

Sharpe's Company Chicken Liver Toast

Easy to prepare, this dish makes a fantastic antipasto

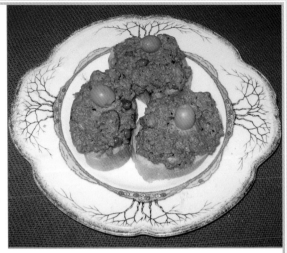

To cover 8 slices you will need:
570g (20oz) chicken liver
8 anchovy fillets
113g (8 tbsp) capers
120ml ($\frac{1}{2}$ cup) chicken stock
pinch of pepper and chilli powder

Finely chop the chicken livers and anchovy fillets; lightly sauté in butter and then add the chicken stock to the pan and let them cook completely. Add the capers and a bit of butter; stir gently to combine. Allow the mixture to simmer gently long enough for the flavours to combine; do not allow it to reach a boil. Add a pinch of freshly ground pepper and a pinch of chilli powder; spread on toasted bread to serve.

Mungo's Mouthwatering Mushroom Caps

Surrounded by the often arid and barren landscape of the Iberian Peninsula, Major Mungo Munro pined for his misty highland homeland. While playing his bagpipes he might well have longed for a treat like this, featuring fungi that grow wild in his native Scotland.

To make 3 dozen you will need:
900g (32oz) white mushrooms
450g (16oz) cream cheese, softened
500g (1 lb) bacon
113g ($\frac{1}{2}$ cup or 1 stick) margarine or butter

Cook bacon and crumble into a bowl with the softened cream cheese. Gently remove the stem from the mushrooms. Dice the stems and lightly sauté in margarine. Then mix with the cream cheese and bacon. Lightly sauté the caps on both sides; place on paper towel and dab to remove extra margarine. Place caps on a baking sheet, top side down. Spoon filling into the caps and place under the grill for 10 minutes.

SALADS, SOUPS & EGGS

Overheard around the riflemen's campfire

"Dan – I've met this girl – as far as I can make out, she wants to make me supper – but what's 'salad'?"

"I've heard of it lad. Think the officers' ladies have it sometimes. It's vegetables;
things like onions, cabbage or lettuce and such."

"How long does that take to boil then, Dan?"

"No lad – you don't boil it, or even roast it, you just slice it up."

"Eat it without cooking! But Dan, we ain't animals!"

It is to be feared that the soldiers had not heard of healthy eating. But as we do not take those lovely long walks they so enjoyed all over Spain and Portugal, we'd better pay more attention to salads. And these are so delicious that even a young rifleman may have enjoyed them.

Apple & Potato Salad

This probably took Dan Hagman back to thoughts of his youth in Cheshire.
Days of scrumping in orchards and raiding vegetable patches on his way back from poaching expeditions.
Days when he enjoyed the crunch of a crisp apple. Days when he had teeth!

To serve 4-6 you will need:
About 5 cold, boiled potatoes (the harder waxy types are best)
2 apples, cored and chopped
125ml ($1/2$ cup) mayonnaise
Finely chopped parsley
2 sticks celery, chopped
A little finely chopped mint
1 small red onion – very finely sliced or chopped

Combine all ingredients and chill.

Garbanzo Bean Salad, Two Ways

Wash and drain garbanzo beans, cook overnight in a slow cooker (crockpot) with plenty of water. Cook until the beans are completely tender (undercooked beans are difficult to digest, to put it gently).

Remove the beans to a salad bowl using a slotted spoon, while beans are hot, dress with salt, pepper and plenty of extra virgin olive oil. Remove a portion of the beans, and serve to children (or adults) who do not like the other salad ingredients. (It is amazing how many of these simply dressed garbanzo beans a child can eat.)

Add to the rest of the garbanzo beans some diced cucumbers, tomatoes, red onions, all cut about the size of a garbanzo bean, and some pitted, sliced olives (I like Kalamata olives), add some red wine vinegar and perhaps more extra virgin olive oil; toss well. Some chopped parsley is nice too if you have it. Serve to the grown-ups.

Hagman's Best Vinegar Slaw

This recipe is good Southern American country cooking. Not Hagman's area of the world to be sure, but I bet he'd like it, just the same.

To serve 4-6 you will need:
1 head cabbage, shredded
170g ($3/4$ cup) sugar
apple cider vinegar
5g (1 tsp) salt
2.5g ($1/2$ tsp) pepper

Fill medium bowl with sugar, salt, and pepper.

Pour in enough vinegar to just cover the sugar. Do not stir. Let combination sit for 1 to $1 1/2$ hours; pour over shredded cabbage and allow mixture to seep into cabbage.

Chill for 30 minutes; serve.

Harper's Sweet & Hot Onion Salad

To serve 4-6 you will need to mix:
120ml ($^1/_2$ cup) olive oil
30ml (2 tbsp) red wine vinegar
30ml (2 tbsp) lemon juice
2g ($^1/_2$ tsp) dried oregano
2g ($^1/_2$ tsp) dried marjoram
5g (1 tsp) red chilli pepper flakes
30g (2 tbsp) drained capers (optional)
salt and white pepper to taste

Pour the mixture over:
2 large thin sweet sliced onions (red onion can be used)
230g (8oz) sliced black olives

Add:
230g (8oz) Feta cheese, crumbled
Cover and refrigerate overnight. Serve on a bed of shredded lettuce and tomato slices.

Osteoporosis literally means "porous bones."

Heavenly Seven Layer Salad

To serve 6-8 you will need:
1 head lettuce, shredded
450g (2 cups) tomatoes, chopped
450g (2 cups) sliced mushrooms
280g (10oz) frozen peas, thawed and drained
113g (4oz) Cheddar cheese, grated
1 large sweet or red onion, sliced and separated into rings
475ml (2 cups) salad dressing, such as mayonnaise
bacon bits

In a 2L (2 quart) serving bowl, layer the lettuce, tomatoes, mushrooms, peas, cheese, and onions.

Spread salad dressing over the top, sealing to edge of bowl; cover.

Chill several hours or overnight. Garnish with bacon bits.

The Rifles' Green Spinach Salad

Rich in calcium, this refreshing side salad goes well with cold chicken and beef dishes.

To serve 2 you will need:

1 large handful of fresh, washed, well-drained spinach (not frozen)
1/4 small white cabbage
1 small red pepper
1 small green pepper
1 small yellow or orange pepper
2 medium onions (sweet ones if possible) or red ones would look pretty
2 medium carrots
6g (1 tsp) caster sugar
60 - 75ml (4 - 5 tbsp) French dressing
salt and pepper
Chopped parsley or coriander to garnish

Finely shred the washed, drained spinach and cabbage. Peel, halve and finely slice the onions.

De-seed the peppers and slice finely (these can be charred and skinned first for anyone who finds the skins hard to digest).

Wash, peel and finely slice the carrots. Put all the vegetables into a large serving bowl and mix well. Keep in the refrigerator until ready to serve. To make the dressing, put the sugar, salt, pepper and French dressing in a jam jar, screw on the lid firmly and shake until well mixed. Pour over the vegetables and toss well. Sprinkle with the chopped herbs and serve immediately on a bed of baby spinach leaves.

Hogan's Potato Salad

The straining waistcoat of Wellington's spymaster suggests that he rarely missed a meal, despite his many duties and the privations of the campaign. As a proud Irishman, odds are Hogan would have been able to secure a potato or two to make this salad.

To serve 1 you will need:

250g (8oz) jacket potatoes
2-3 spring onions
1/2 red sweet pepper
1/2 cucumber

For the sauce:
60ml (4 tbsp) sour cream
30ml (2 tbsp) aromatic vinegar (herbs)
15ml (1 tbsp) prepared medium hot mustard
5g (1 tsp) sugar
salt
black pepper

Cook the potatoes; peel when cooked, cool and cube. Dice the onions, pepper, and cucumber into large, evenly sized chunks. Mix everything, adding some milk if necessary.

Prepare the sauce by mixing all the ingredients. Toss with the vegetables and let the salad rest for at least 6 hours; add seasoning if necessary.

Beer Battle Soup

Simple to prepare, this beer based soup makes a filling meal any time of the year.

To serve 3-4 you will need:
680g (1½ lbs) beef rump roast, cut in 2.5cm (1 inch) cubes
1 large onion, diced
1g (¼ tsp) dried sage
1g (¼ tsp) dried thyme
1g (¼ tsp) garlic powder
0.5g (⅛ tsp) white pepper
710ml (3 cups) Guinness beer
355 ml (1½ cup) water
rustic brown bread

Heat a large saucepan on medium high heat; add the beef and sear on all sides. Turn the heat down to medium and add the onion and the herbs. Continue cooking until the onions are translucent, but not browning. Turn the heat down to low and add the liquids. Simmer for a minimum of 30 minutes.

To serve: In a soup bowl place a slice of bread and ladle in the soup.

Tips: You may add your choice of chopped vegetables at the same time as the onions. I recommend Guinness because it has the body to hold up in this recipe. Most other beers would be lost.

Vegetable Soup Lucille

To serve 4-6 you will need:
Dice the following into bite-size pieces:
4 carrots, scraped
2 small white turnips, peeled
2 medium potatoes, peeled
1 large stack celery
9 cloves garlic, peeled and crushed
brown the vegetables in olive oil and add:
1.9L (8 cups) water
salt and pepper to taste

Turn the heat up and bring to a boil, then lower to medium heat and cook until vegetables are done, about 15 to 20 minutes.

Add 113g (½ cup) canned or frozen green peas. Cook 10 minutes longer.

To serve place one or two thick slices of the bread of your choice in a bowl and ladle soup over it. Top with grated Cheddar cheese or cheese of your choice.

Sharpe's Duchess Soup

Pumpkin Celery Soup with Salmon Caviar

The recipe was contributed by a friend of mine, Birgit Damer, a prize-winning cook. She created it and liked the idea of our cookbook so much that I was allowed to give it a "Sharpe" name.

To serve 4-6 you will need:
3 heads of celery (finely chopped)
1 small pumpkin
2 cloves of garlic
fresh ginger root
1ltr (4 cups) coconut milk
$^1/_2$ ltr (2 cups) cream
at least $^1/_2$ ltr (2 cups) concentrated vegetable stock
85g (3oz) truffle butter
fresh peppercorns
mace
salmon roe
Optional - 1 bunch of parsley stems 'chips' - chopped into pieces and fried in oil

Finely chop the garlic and a comparable amount of ginger and sweat in a large saucepan with the truffle butter.

Carve out the pumpkin flesh and chop into small pieces. Add the chopped celery, pumpkin and vegetable stock, and simmer together with the coconut milk and the cream until all the ingredients are soft and can be pureed. Do not allow the mixture to come to the boil.

Blend the soup in a blender (a hand-held blender will suffice) until the soup is creamy. Season to taste with pepper and mace, and garnish with salmon roe.

Add fried parsley stem 'chips' if desired and serve with chunks of SA Bread (see page 76).

Slow Cooker Split Pea Soup

To serve 4-6 you will need:

370g (13oz) dried green split peas, rinsed
1 hambone or hock or 450g (2 cups) diced ham
3 carrots, peeled and sliced
1 medium onion, chopped
2 stalks celery, chopped
1 bay leaf
60g (¼ cup) fresh parsley
salt, pepper to taste
1L (4 cups) hot water.

Layer ingredients in the slow cooker. Pour in water. Cover and cook on low for 8 to 10 hours (high for 4 to 5 hours) until peas are very tender and ham is falling off the bone.

Remove bones and bay leaf and serve garnished with croutons.

Tip: After removing the bones and bay leaf put the soup through the food processor – that way you don't have to worry too much about chopping everything too carefully when preparing the soup!

General Calvet's Sweet Potato-Crab Bisque

To serve 8-10 you will need:

2.3kg (5 lbs) dark red sweet potatoes, peeled and diced
1 large onion, minced
30g (2 tbsp) butter or oil
950ml (1 qt) chicken stock
950ml (1qt) water
5g (1 tsp) cayenne pepper, or to taste
14g (1 tbsp) fresh ginger, grated
5g (1 tsp) salt, or 9g (2 tsp) Kosher salt
30ml (2 tbsp) tomato paste
2g (½ tsp) freshly ground nutmeg, or to taste
2g (½ tsp) freshly ground black pepper, or to taste
475ml (2 cups) heavy cream or ½ and ½
950ml (4 cups) milk, or more depending on consistency
227g (8oz) crab, picked through and shredded – or 450g (1 lb) imitation crab, flaked and finely chopped

General Calvet was a French enemy who became a friend. He was as famous for his appetite as for his fighting abilities and he enjoyed a considerable variety of food. On the horrific retreat from Moscow the whole French army was starvation stricken. Calvet ate his corporal.

After Napoleon's final downfall, Calvet left Europe and settled in Louisiana, where he developed a real taste for this seafood treat. Don't worry, it contains no corporal meat! But this dish may go well with fava beans and a nice chianti…

Put oil or butter into a large stock pot. Add onion, cayenne, salt, nutmeg and black pepper. Sweat onions slowly until translucent; do not allow to brown.

Add peeled and diced sweet potatoes and cover with stock and water.

Cook until tender and purée with immersion blender or in regular blender until smooth. Stir in cream, milk and crab.

Heat only until the soup is hot; do not boil. Adjust seasonings and serve with crusty sourdough bread.

Perkins' Adventurous Eggs

Varying the amount of chilli will determine just how adventurous a dish you will have! This would make a good camp fire meal, using "liberated" eggs and the flavours would, perhaps, remind Richard of his service in India.

Heat the olive oil in a large, heavy frying pan and gently fry the shallots or onions, peppers and garlic for about 10 minutes, without browning. Add the chilli, cumin, oregano, peas, beans and tomatoes and mix well. Add the chilli sauce to taste. Increase the heat and cook, uncovered, for another 10 minutes or until the mixture has thickened. Season with salt and pepper. Break the eggs on top of the mixture and sprinkle over the cheese. Cover the frying pan with a lid or foil. Lower the heat and barely simmer for 10 - 15 minutes until the eggs are cooked to your liking. Sprinkle over the coriander or parsley and serve straight from the pan with lots of bread to mop up the juice.

To serve 4 you will need:
45ml (3 tbsp) light olive oil
2 shallots or 1 small onion, finely chopped
3 cloves garlic, crushed
1/2 green pepper, finely chopped
1/2 red pepper, finely chopped
handful of green beans, blanched and cut into chunks
handful of green peas, fresh or frozen
6 large, really ripe tomatoes, skinned and cut into chunks or 400g (14oz can) of tomatoes
4 eggs
1 small fresh red chilli, deseeded and finely chopped
4g (1 tsp) fresh oregano chopped or 1g (1/4 tsp) dried oregano
2g (1/2 tsp) ground cumin
chilli sauce to taste
113g (1/2 cup) Manchega or Cheddar cheese, grated
freshly chopped coriander or parsley to garnish
salt and pepper to taste

Unlike other Army regiments, the officers of the Rifle brigades would regularly dine with their men; and so became familiar with each soldier under their command.

Chinese Tea Eggs

Enough chickens survived in Spain and Portugal to provide eggs for an occasional treat, and as the soldiers were so addicted to their cups of tea, that ingredient was always available. It often had an unusual quality about it; a slight taint of gunpowder because men kept the loose tealeaves in their ammunition pouches to keep it dry, and this may have added a certain piquancy to the recipe!

You're going to need:
12 eggs
9g (2 tsp) salt
60ml (¼ cup) soy sauce
5g (1 tsp) sugar
5g (1 tsp) loose tea leaves,
or 1 tea bag
1 whole star anise
1 cinnamon stick, 5cm (2 inches) long

Put eggs in a large saucepan, cover with cold water and bring to the boil. Turn heat to low, cover and simmer for 10 minutes. Drain and then run cold water over the eggs.

Lightly crack eggs all over, but do not peel. Put eggs back in the saucepan, cover with cold water, add all the other ingredients; bring to a boil. Turn heat to low, cover and simmer for another 10 minutes. Turn off heat and allow the eggs to cool in the flavoured tea. Refrigerate.

The longer the eggs sit in the flavoured tea, the saltier and more flavourful they become. Warm over low heat before serving.

Lucille's Quiche Lorraine

To serve 4 you will need:
113g (½ cup) butter
227g (1 cup) flour
1 egg
120ml (½ cup) cold water

Filling:
4-5 slices of ham, cooked and diced
2-3 slices of bacon, cooked and diced
284g (1¼ cup) Swiss cheese, grated
(preferably Gruyère or any other spicy sort)

Preheat oven to 200°C/Gas Mark 6/400°F

Knead ingredients into a dough and let it rest for about 30 minutes in the refrigerator, then spread in a 25cm round dish (10 inch), making sure to cover the sides of the dish as well. Spread the filling over the dough.

Carefully mix and spread over the filling:
1 egg
118ml (½ cup) cream
(crème fraiche or milk)
Black pepper to taste

Bake for about 30 minutes. Best served hot with chilled dry white wine or champagne.

Salamanca Cheese Soufflé

While Sharpe was recovering in Salamanca from the near fatal wound inflicted by the dastardly Colonel Leroux, he needed careful nursing. La Marquesa wanted him fully restored (she had her reasons!) and provided the house in which he could regain his strength. She would also have wanted to ensure that his appetite was stimulated, and easily digested nourishing dishes such as this soufflé would have been ideal. It must have worked – Sharpe was soon getting his revenge upon the villainous Leroux…

To serve 2 you will need:
3 eggs
28g (2 tbsp) butter
14g 1 tbsp) plain flour
118ml (1/2 cup) milk
85g (6 tbsp) strong, mature Cheddar cheese, finely grated
1g (1/4 tsp) dried mustard
salt and pepper
extra butter for greasing the dish
a little grated Parmesan cheese

Preheat oven to 200°C/Gas Mark 6/400°F

Grease a 15 or 18cm (6 or 7 inch) soufflé dish with a little butter. Shake in some very finely grated Parmesan cheese, moving the dish so that it is lightly coated. Separate the eggs, and beat the whites until stiff. Melt the butter and stir in the flour and mustard, making a smooth roux. Add the milk slowly and bring the liquid up to simmering point, stirring all the time. Keep stirring until the liquid thickens and is smooth.

Remove from the heat and let the liquid cool a little (or you risk setting the egg yolks as you add them). Add the cheese, seasoning and then the eggs yolks, a little at a time. Beat it well to make the mixture smooth.

Add just one tablespoon of your stiffly beaten egg white and beat again, to slacken the mixture. Then, with a metal spoon, gently fold in the rest of the beaten egg white.

Pour the mixture carefully into the prepared soufflé dish and bake in the centre of the oven for about 20 minutes. Do not open the oven door until at least 15 minutes of the cooking time have gone. If you want to check it at that point, then open the door carefully, and don't slam it closed should more time be required, or you risk the soufflé collapsing. The soufflé is done if it is well-risen, golden brown on top and feels slightly firm when pressed gently. Serve it at once with a green salad.

Cauldron Cooking

In the earliest examples of homes, the fire was in the centre of the floor and food was prepared in a wide variety of ways. A trench could have been dug and food placed on hot stones to be cooked. Alternatively a metal pot could have been suspended over the fire and various food items placed in the pot would all have cooked together to produce a sort of stew. The influence of the Roman occupation of Britain can be found in one form of food preparation, cauldron cooking.

The word cauldron derives from the Latin *caldarium*, which means hot bath. Put very simply, various items of food were placed in hot water and left to cook. Various food historians have suggested that the liquid that was left in the cauldron after the meat and vegetables were removed stayed there and that additional food was added day after day. If the heat was sufficient the food would boil, and no harm would come to those who would eat its contents. Cauldron cookery would probably have been found in every cottage in England if the occupants could afford to purchase a cauldron. The cauldron would have hung over the fire in the kitchen with food bubbling away in it.

Cottagers developed various ways of using the cauldron for cooking, using different methods to separate and hold foods so that they would cook separately in hot water. Puddings could be wrapped in a cloth, meat suspended from twigs or metal prongs and a horizontal board that would fit in the cauldron could be used to create a separate cooking area. These can vary enormously. A farmhouse, by the mid fifteenth century might have, as well as the open fire place, a brick built bread oven, and this would have changed how food was prepared to a certain extent. Temperature was adjusted by the size of the fire and the type of fuel used. A cook needed to know which type of wood burnt well and provided the most heat. Green wood, that is wood that has just been cut, will contain more water than seasoned wood. It sends out white smoke, almost like steam, and so the heat is not as intense. Seasoned wood, especially if kept dry, will burn more fiercely and so gives out more heat. The type of wood was also important; the heavier the wood, the better the heat.

The cauldron could also be moved closer to the fire, or suspended further away from it to control the temperature. This form of food preparation was common in England for many centuries and would have influenced soldiers, like Sharpe and the Chosen Men, who suddenly found they had to prepare their own food when they were away from home.

During the Peninsular wars, soldiers either had food supplied and prepared for them by the Commissariat, or, when regiments like the Rifle Brigade came into being, had to forage for themselves. Unlike the French, who encouraged soldiers to commandeer needed supplies, Wellington had very strict rules and all goods had to be paid for by the soldiers. Taking any food from the indigenous population was strictly forbidden and punishable by hanging. In some areas of the Peninsula there was very little food to be found, and the soldiers would have to improvise meals for themselves. A cauldron, set on the fire with some root vegetables, would make a good soup and there were ways of improving the meat content. Small slivers of wood placed along the lip of the cauldron acted as bridges along which an adventurous mouse or rat would wander. When they reached the end of the bridge, they would over balance and fall into the cauldron. The result was a small but important addition of protein to an otherwise nutritionally insufficient diet.

Looking up the chimney of a cottage built c1600. The metal struts that probably held the chains and jacks for the cauldron are still in place.

"Beechwood fires burn bright and clear
If the logs are kept a year
Store your beech for Christmastide
With new holly laid beside
Chestnuts only good they say
If for years tis stayed away
Birch and firwood burn too fast
Blaze too bright and do not last
Flames from larch will shoot up high
Dangerously the sparks will fly
But Ashwood green and Ashwood brown
Are fit for a Queen with a golden crown
Oaken logs, if dry and old
Keep away the winters cold
Poplar gives a bitter smoke
Fills your eyes and makes you choke
Elmwood burns like churchyard mould
Even the very flames burn cold
Hawthorn bakes the sweetest bread
So it is in Ireland said
Applewood will scent the room
Pears wood smells like a flower in bloom
But Ashwood wet and Ashwood dry
A King may warm his slippers by.

Cauldron cooking had another aspect to it, especially for men who were away from their main regiment and who had to rely on each other. Eating from a communal pot would have helped to form relationships between the men. They had to depend on and trust each other with a very basic human need. Additionally, what went into the pot would depend on the time of year and the location the men found themselves in. Food was seasonal and although some foods could be stored, this was not an option for men who were constantly on the move. Finally, season, trust and luck were augmented by the two essentials necessary for cooking in the open; the ability to light a fire and keep it going, and maintaining a small store of salt for flavouring.

Cauldron cooking can be seen at many re-enactment meetings and the smell that comes from the food being cooked is often mouth watering - and possibly misleading! It is doubtful if re-enactment groups have to forage for their food or look for suitable wood. Many of the men who had to survive in the open would eat what ever they could find or buy because that was the only way they would be able to survive. Today, food preparation is a skill that soldiers use in modern armies; and the nearest equivalent to the Rifles are possibly Special Forces. These modern day warriors have evolved their own methods of food preparation and new ingredients are used, and if Special Forces may not relish the contents of a cauldron from Peninsular times, it is equally doubtful that the Chosen Men would have enjoyed a worm omelette!

Main Courses

Main Courses

One of the biggest problems for Wellington's Army was provisioning. It was extremely expensive, consumed financial resources only grudgingly allocated by the government back in London, and sometimes dictated the tactics Wellington was forced to adopt. The Battle of Talavera was a brilliant victory, but was followed by a retreat to Portugal, as the British Army could not be fed in Spain at this time.

The French tried to overcome the food problem by seizing supplies from the local population – and were thus hated and helped to provoke the bitter guerrilla war by the Spanish Partisans. More French soldiers died in this than were killed by the British, Portuguese and Spanish armies.

For the troops, the situation was clear enough – supplies often failed to get through or were of very poor quality. The huge 'Flanders Cauldrons' often had a little rancid meat, padded out with whatever the soldiers could provide. The hard twice-baked bread of the campaign marches provided little enjoyment, but at least made sure that hunger did not weaken the troops.
Of course, the daily ration of rum also helped to keep up morale!

Sharpe's Chosen Men would have fared better than most. Dan Hagman's poaching experience and his accuracy with the Baker rifle was no doubt invaluable. Looting was punishable by death, and so bartering a few cartridges to the local people, or sweet-talking a few of the girls, might prove useful. Possibly Rifleman Harris's fluency in Spanish and Portuguese meant that the Chosen Men rarely went short of food – and if those local girls caught sight of a certain green-clad, green-eyed officer, how could they resist giving their all for the war effort….?

Hogan's Company Potatoes

Major Hogan was a sociable man, and could use his fluency in Spanish and Portuguese to charm the disgruntled ladies in whose homes he might find himself billeted. Some of them found themselves being instructed in the niceties of Irish cooking, and even enjoyed it!

He loved potato dishes, and this would have been a particular favourite, and could be guaranteed to attract the company of Sharpe and Harper. On such occasions, Sharpe became an honorary Irishman!
Now if only they could locate some Irish whisky to accompany it…

To serve 12 you will need:
4-5 large jacket potatoes, peeled and coarsely grated
450g (2 cups) grated Cheddar cheese
28g (2 tbsp) parsley, chopped
28g (2 tbsp) spring onions, chopped
1g ($^1/_4$ tsp) salt
1g ($^1/_4$ tsp) pepper
237ml (1 cup) half and half cream
450g (2 cups) grated Gruyère
Paprika for garnish

Examination of skeletons from a working class section of 18th century London revealed virtually no evidence of osteoporosis in post-menopausal women, despite a relatively poor diet. Scientists believe the major contributing factor to their bone health was the amount of weight-bearing exercise they performed on a daily basis!

Preheat oven to 260°C/Gas Mark 9/500°F

In a large bowl, combine all ingredients, except Gruyère and paprika.

Place mixture in a 33 x 23 cm (13 x 9 inch) that has been coated with non-stick cooking spray. Sprinkle potato mixture with Gruyère and paprika then bake for 45 minutes, until golden.

Serve hot.

Challenge Shoe-peg Sweetcorn

This is a very simple corn recipe that tastes like fried corn without all the work.

To serve 4-6 you will need:
570g (2 1/2 cups) tinned white shoe-peg sweetcorn
85g (6 tbsp) butter
28g (2 tbsp) flour
237ml (1 cup) heavy cream

Preheat oven to 180°C/Gas Mark 4/350°F

Drain sweetcorn and put in a casserole dish. Melt butter and stir to add flour; pour over the sweetcorn.

Pour the whipping cream over the sweetcorn. Cover and bake for 1 hour.

"Couldn't Catch the Chicken" Ratatouille

Ratatouille is a traditional French dish that is quick and easy to make; indeed, Lucille could have easily finished the preparation before Richard managed to catch the chicken for the evening meal. It's also very filling – important when your English soldier comes in from the barnyard empty-handed! The spices and chillies in this version give the dish a taste of the American southwest.

To serve 4-6 you will need:
1 medium aubergine – cut into 2.5cm (1 inch) cubes
2 large onions, coarsely chopped
1 garlic clove, crushed
80ml (1/3 cup) olive oil
2 or 3 green, red, or yellow peppers, coarsely chopped
1 or 2 courgettes, cut into 2cm (3/4 inch) slices
1g (1/4 tsp) oregano
1g (1/4 tsp) coriander
1g (1/4 tsp) basil, ground
1g (1/4 tsp) cumin, powdered
177ml (3/4 cup) tinned tomato paste
340g (1 1/2 cups) tinned, chopped tomatoes
227g (1 cup) tinned mild or hot green chillies, drained
salt & pepper to taste

In a large, heavy-bottom pot with a good lid (a pressure cooker works well – no need to pressurise), heat the olive oil and cook onion, garlic, and peppers over medium heat until soft.

Add aubergine and cook, stirring often, until aubergine is brown. Add the remaining ingredients; stir. Cover the pot and continue cooking until the vegetables are soft and the flavours melded – about 30 minutes.

Serve hot or cold.

Curried Carrots

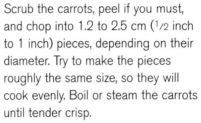

To serve 4 you will need:
1 large, 2 medium, or 3 small carrots per person (between 4 and 12 carrots)
60g (1/4 cup) butter
60g (1/4 cup) brown sugar, packed
your favourite prepared curry powder or paste, to taste
ginger - powder or paste, to taste
salt and pepper
a handful of chopped nuts - walnuts or pecans are good
a handful of raisins, sultanas, currants or chopped dates

Scrub the carrots, peel if you must, and chop into 1.2 to 2.5 cm (1/2 inch to 1 inch) pieces, depending on their diameter. Try to make the pieces roughly the same size, so they will cook evenly. Boil or steam the carrots until tender crisp.
Do NOT overcook – there is little in life you can do to ruin a carrot except overcooking it into a tough, soggy orange lump.

In a large skillet, melt the butter over low heat. Add the brown sugar; stir constantly until the sugar dissolves and the mix is bubbling. Add the curry, ginger, and salt and pepper to taste. I use a moderately spicy curry powder, starting with 5 g (1 tsp) and adding more if I feel like it, and dry, powdered ginger, about 1.25 to 2.5 g (1/4 to 1/2 tsp) in total — again, it depends on your taste.

Add the carrots to the pan and coat with the mix. Turn up the heat and continue cooking the carrots, keeping them moving, until they just begin to brown — this takes about 3 or 4 minutes. Add the fruit and nuts, if desired; shake the pan to distribute them throughout. Serve immediately. I make this dish last when preparing a meal - it is very quick and tastes best steaming hot!

Rocket Troop Baked Beans

Labour-intensive but worth it. Don't forget to start soaking the beans the night before!

To serve 4-6 you will need:
454g (1 lb) dry beans
1g (1/4 tsp) baking soda
2g (1/2 tsp) salt
2g (1/2 tsp) mustard
60ml (1/4 cup) molasses
pinch pepper
1 medium onion, chopped
10ml (2 tsp) vinegar
15g (1 tbsp) brown sugar
120ml (1/2 cup) ketchup
OPTIONAL: 115g (1/4 lb) salt pork

Soak beans overnight. In the morning add baking soda to beans and bring to a boil, then simmer until the beans are cooked (the time varies depending on the type of beans you choose to use). Save the cooking water!

Put cooked beans and other ingredients into an oven-proof pot (a proper stoneware bean pot works best); mix together. Add cooking water to cover the mixture; cook at 130°C/Gas Mark 1/2/250°F for 7 hours. After 4 hours, remove 1 cup of beans from the pot and mash. Stir back into remaining beans carefully. Add more cooking water if beans start to dry out.

"Best Shot" Hagman's Baked Stuffed Tomatoes

To serve 5 you will need:
5 medium sized fresh, ripe tomatoes

Preheat oven to 170°C/Gas Mark 3/325°F

Slice off the top of the tomatoes; scoop out the tomato pulp and set it aside. Sprinkle salt on the inside of tomatoes and turn them upside down on a plate to drain. Chop the tomato pulp and set aside; reserve any juice separately.

Add:
340g (1¹/₂ cups) plain bread crumbs
reserved tomato juice and enough hot water to make 180ml (³/₄ cup) liquid

Stir into the stuffing until melted:
85g (6 tbsp) room temperature cream cheese
salt and pepper to taste

To make the stuffing:
sauté in 120ml (¹/₂ cup) olive oil:
30g (2 tbsp) garlic, minced
115g (¹/₂ cup) onion, chopped
add and continue cooking for 10 minutes:
400g (1³/₄ cups) frozen chopped spinach, defrosted (pack tightly when measuring)
reserved tomato pulp
120ml (¹/₂ cup) Worcestershire sauce or Henderson's relish

Arrange the tomatoes on a foil covered baking tin and generously fill each shell with the stuffing mix. Bake 25 to 30 minutes; remove from the oven and top each tomato with a slice of Mozzarella cheese. Return to the oven for 3 to 5 minutes until cheese is melted. Serve hot.

Sautéed Aubergine (Eggplant)

This dish is a wonderful side dish with Macaroni al Tonno!

To serve 2 you will need:
1 aubergine
10ml (2 tsp) olive oil
fresh basil
60ml (¹/₄ cup) vegetable stock

Cut the aubergine into small pieces and sauté in the oil; add the vegetable stock and basil and simmer for about 10 minutes. Serve hot.

Schnitzel Beans Lossow

The generous German Captain who saved Sharpe's hide on more than one occasion might also have taught our hero how to make this simple and delicious vegetable dish.

To serve 4-6 you will need:

850g (28oz) tinned green beans, drained or 681g (24oz) fresh
4 slices bacon, chopped
227g (1 cup) sugar
118ml (1/2 cup) white vinegar
1 small onion, chopped

Fry chopped bacon until brown; add sugar, onion, and vinegar to bacon and grease. Cook until sugar is dissolved. Add beans; simmer 20 minutes. Sauce is also good on other vegetables.

KGL Kugel

In 1803 Napoleon imposed peace and the Electorate of Hanover was dissolved. King George III was also the Elector of Hanover and it was only natural that many former Hanoverian soldiers fled to Britain. These veterans together with other levied soldiers were formed into the King's German Legion later that same year. While kugel is a Jewish staple it has its culinary and linguistic roots in Germany, so a simple savoury casserole like this one could well have been on the menu in a KGL mess.

To serve 4 you will need:

60g (1/4 cup) green pepper, chopped
230g (1 cup) onion, chopped
115g (1/2 cup) celery, chopped
340g (11/2 cup) carrots, grated
285g (10 oz) frozen chopped spinach, thawed
3 eggs, beaten
7g (11/2 tsp) salt
2g (1/2 tsp) pepper
170g (3/4 cup) matzo meal (or substitute very fine bread crumbs)

Preheat oven to 180°C/Gas Mark 4/350°F
Sauté raw vegetables in a little olive oil; add thawed spinach and heat through. In a large bowl combine vegetables, eggs, salt, pepper and matzo meal. Turn into a greased baking dish and bake for 1 hour or until done in the middle. Cut into squares and serve.

The NOS recommends a balanced diet to strengthen and protect your bones. Consuming too much meat, cheese and grain foods may upset the acid balance within your body, leaching calcium from your bones.
Counteract the negative effects by eating plenty of fruit and veg – they will help keep your body's acid balance stable.

Squash Casserole

To serve 6-8 you will need:

6 medium yellow squash
1 onion, chopped
115g (1/2 cup) sour cream
115g (1/2 cup) grated Cheddar cheese
12 salted cream crackers
or saltines, crushed
salt and pepper to taste

Preheat oven to 180°C/Gas Mark 4/350°F

Cut squash in chunks; cook until soft; drain. Mash with potato masher and drain again. Mix squash with other ingredients except crackers; spread in lightly greased casserole dish. Sprinkle crackers over top, sprinkle more cheese over crackers if desired, and spray top with cooking spray.

Bake for 30 to 40 minutes.

47

PASTA

It was as the Chosen Men were whiling away time in Cadiz, waiting for Sharpe's orders about some dangerous mission, that they encountered pasta for the first time. It was not an army staple: it just turned up in the box of supplies dropped off by Sergeant Harper.

Cooper and Perkins were unpacking the food, and were puzzled by this weird looking item. Luckily, Harris, as usual, was a mine of information.

"It's pasta, lads. Comes from Italy. You use it a bit like we use potatoes or rice – it goes with meat and such. Just boil it. This kind is called spaghetti."

They weren't entirely convinced. And if they hadn't been so concerned with examining this odd stuff, they might have noticed the gleam in Harris's eyes as he continued,

"There's field upon field of the stuff growing in Italy. Some kinds grow on trees. It all has to have the outer shells removed – done by girls rubbing it up and down their thighs."

Harris wandered off – the girl he'd met in the tavern last night had been very friendly, and he wondered about the suitability of her thighs for spaghetti threshing….
Cooper and Perkins became strangely enthusiastic and decided to be adventurous with tonight's meal.

"Well, Coops, let's boil it then. An hour should be enough. Still looks a bit weird though. Shall we have it mashed?"

Horse Guards' Broccoli & Spinach Lasagne

Wellington must often have thought he was fighting two major wars, not one. The war against the French was pretty straightforward compared to the hidden war. In this, there were two enemies; the Spaniards to whom the idea of Wellington leading the allied armies was anathema and the political enemies at home. The most dangerous of these were the enemies at Horse Guards, who administered the Army. Sinecured officials at Horse Guards frequently saddled Wellington with useless pomposities as officers, such as Sir Henry Simmerson and Sir Augustus Farthingdale.

They also wasted much of the money which was needed to provide the troops with adequate provisions. They would have loved to have thought of ways to satisfy soldiers' appetites without so much of that expensive beef. Now if only they'd had access to this recipe, the beef ration could have stretched much further and the whole army could have been fed both healthily and cheaply…

To serve 4-6 you will need:
6 sheets of ready-to-use lasagne
60g (2oz) Cheddar cheese, grated
30g (2 tbsp) Parmesan cheese,
freshly grated
113g (4oz) frozen spinach, thawed and
well drained
113g (4oz) frozen broccoli, thawed,
briefly blanched in boiling water to soften
slightly, well drained
120ml (½ cup) double cream

For the meat sauce:
1 medium onion, finely chopped
1 clove garlic, crushed
113g (½ cup) mushrooms, finely sliced
450g (1 lb) lean minced beef
880g (30 oz) tinned chopped tomatoes
2.5g (½ tsp) oregano
5g (1 tsp) sugar
salt and pepper

For the cheese sauce:
60g (2oz) butter
60g (¼ cup) plain flour
475 ml (2 cups) milk
113g (½ cup) Cheddar cheese, grated
14g (1 tbsp) Parmesan cheese,
freshly grated
pinch of nutmeg
salt and pepper

Preheat oven to 180°C/Gas Mark 4/350°F

Make the meat sauce by browning the minced beef in a heavy pan. Add the onion, garlic and mushrooms; cook until the onion is soft but not brown. Add the tomatoes, oregano and sugar, and season with salt and pepper. Cover and simmer gently for 35-45 minutes, then uncover and cook for a further 10-15 minutes until the sauce has thickened.

Make the cheese sauce. Melt the butter, add the flour and stir until smooth. Cook for 1 minute then add the salt, pepper and nutmeg. Gradually add the milk and stir until thickened. Add the grated Cheddar and Parmesan cheeses and stir until melted into the sauce.

To assemble the lasagne, briefly soak the pasta sheets in hot water to soften slightly. Then place two sheets in the base of a lightly oiled oven-proof dish. Spread with half the meat sauce and then half the cheese sauce. Place the spinach in a layer over the cheese sauce and top with two more sheets of pasta. Spread these with the rest of the meat and cheese sauces and place the broccoli on top. Cover with remaining pasta sheets and sprinkle with the mixed cheeses. Bake for 25-30 minutes, then drizzle the top with the cream and bake for a further 15 minutes or until golden brown. Let stand for 10 minutes before serving.

Patriotic War Pyrohy (Pierogies)

These freeze very well. To reheat simply thaw and sauté in a pan with butter or olive oil until brown.

Mix all ingredients well and knead until elastic (the dough will be sticky). Brush with oil and let stand 15 minutes. Roll out and cut into circles with pastry cutter or glass. Place filling on dough, fold into half-circles, dampen finger tips and pinch edges well. Place in boiling water, stir with wooden spoon, boil rapidly for 3 minutes. When pyrohy puff up, remove and coat with butter to prevent sticking. Serve as is or sauté until golden brown.

To make 3 dozen you will need:
Dough:
907g (4 cups) flour
414 ml (1¾ cup) warm water
15ml (1 tbsp) oil
1 egg
2g (½ tsp) salt (optional)

Suggested Fillings:
Cheddar cheese & mashed potato
Cottage cheese
Sauerkraut: Sauté sauerkraut in with some chopped onion and olive oil or butter; add caraway seed to taste and a little red wine for colour and flavour. Sauté until very soft, about 45 minutes to 1 hour.
Raw Fruit: Strawberries, raspberries, black cherries, blueberries or any other fruit with a strong flavour. Cook pyrohy as normal, sprinkle with brown sugar and serve warm with whipped cream, ice cream or pancake syrup. Can also be served cold with warm fruit sauces or syrups.

Macaroni Al Tonno

To serve 2 you will need:
1 red chilli pepper, cored and finely chopped
1 onion, finely chopped
2 cloves of garlic, crushed
10ml (2 tsp) olive oil
177ml (¾ cup) vegetable stock
5g (1 tsp) capers, crushed
60g (¼ cup) tinned tuna, in water not oil, drained and flaked
60g (4 tbsp) sour cream
100g (3½ oz) dried macaroni
30g (2 tbsp) chopped parsley

Cook pasta al dente. Heat the oil in a large sauce pan; sauté the garlic, chilli pepper and onion. Add the vegetable stock and let it heat.

Add the capers and tuna; simmer for about 5 minutes. Add sour cream and season to taste.

Mix the sauce with the pasta, sprinkle with parsley and serve with red wine.

Mexican Macaroni & Cheese

To serve 6-8 you will need:
454g (1lb) elbow macaroni, uncooked
454g (2 cups) grated Cheddar cheese
473ml (16oz) salsa

Cook and drain the macaroni according to the package instructions. Mix in the grated cheese and salsa while the macaroni is still hot. Stir until cheese has melted and serve while it is hot.

Pierogi Lasagne

To serve 8-10 you will need:
14 medium potatoes, cooked and mashed
227g (1 cup) cottage cheese
340g (1½ cups) Cheddar cheese, grated
454g (1lb) lasagne sheets
227g (1 cup) butter
227g (½lb) bacon, fried and chopped
454g (2 cups) tinned sauerkraut, drained
2 large onions, chopped

Preheat oven to 180°C
/Gas Mark 4/350°F

Mix the Cheddar cheese, cottage cheese, bacon and sauerkraut into the mashed potatoes. Sauté onions in butter. Layer greased pan with noodles. Spread a layer of the potato mixture over the noodles then spread a layer of onions and butter. Add another layer of noodles, then a layer of potato mixture and a layer of butter and onions. Continue in like fashion until potato mixture is gone. Top with a layer of noodles, then a layer of onions and butter to keep the top moist. Bake for 45 minutes, remove from the oven and allow to stand for 10 minutes. Serve with sautéed onions and sour cream. (Prepare the night before and reheat the next day for easier serving.)

Prawns & Mushroom Pasta

To serve 4-6 you will need:
141g (½ cup) mushrooms, cleaned and sliced
200g (1 cup) butter
141g (5oz) frozen cooked prawns
28g (2 tbsp) flour
227 ml (1 cup) milk
pepper
nutmeg
454g (1lb) dried, short cut pasta (e.g. penne, rigatoni)
200g (1 cup) Parmesan cheese, grated
141g (½ cup) Mozzarella cheese, grated

Preheat oven to 220°C/Gas Mark 7/425°F

Sauté the mushrooms in 28g (2 tbsp) of the butter until soft. Make a sauce with 28g (2 tbsp) of butter, the flour and milk. Season to taste with pepper and grated nutmeg. Stir in the mushrooms, prawns and half of the Parmesan. Cook the pasta for half the length of time given on the packet. Drain well and stir in to the sauce.

Lightly butter an ovenproof dish. Cover the bottom of the dish with one third of the pasta sauce. Sprinkle over one third of the remaining Parmesan and one third of the Mozzarella. Dot with a little of the remaining butter. Add another layer of pasta, then half the remaining cheeses and butter.

Repeat with what is left. Grind some fresh black pepper over the top. Bake for 20 minutes.

FISH

It was as the army marched further inland in Portugal and towards Spain that the soldiers were faced with a challenging Portuguese delicacy, dried salted cod. It travelled well – perhaps too well.

Somehow the Portuguese cooks managed to make a palatable dish from these hard slabs of grey stuff. However, lacking the necessary genetic skills, the British soldiers and their wives soon discovered that the only acceptable recipe seemed to be:

Soak it • Boil it • Taste it • Throw it away…

By the autumn of 1813, the South Essex had reached the north coast of Spain, and for a few months had the easy duty of guarding the supply base of Pasejes. As they waited for Major Sharpe to return from England with the urgently needed new recruits, the Regiment re-discovered the delights of fish fresh from the sea. Soon, they were all feeling much brainier, and Harris, of course, had reached sheer genius level!

We hope the following recipes will have the same beneficial effects for you.

Almond-Stuffed Fish Fillets with Tarragon Sauce

Serve the fillets on a bed of spinach fettuccine for a colorful entrée.

To serve 2 you will need:
114g (1/2 cup) grated Gruyère
56g (4 tbsp) chopped almonds
28g (2 tbsp) snipped chives
28g (2 tbsp) margarine or butter, softened
2 flounder or sole fillets (225g total)
paprika
45ml (3 tbsp) dry white wine
75g (3oz) pasta (such as fettuccine or Linguini), cooked and drained
1 recipe creamy Tarragon sauce

Preheat oven to 190°C/ Gas Mark 5/375°F

For stuffing, mix cheese, almonds, chives, and margarine or butter.

Spoon half of the mixture onto one end of each piece of fish. Roll fish around stuffing. Place fish, seam side down, into small baking dish. Sprinkle with paprika. Pour wine into dish. Bake, uncovered, for 15 minutes or till fish flakes with a fork.

To serve, put pasta onto plate and arrange fish rolls on top.

Serve with creamy Tarragon sauce.

Creamy Tarragon sauce:
57g (¼ cup) grated carrot
14g (1 tbsp) margarine or butter
5g (2 tsp) plain flour
white pepper and salt to taste
a small pinch of dried, crushed Tarragon
120ml (½ cup) milk
57g (¼ cup) grated Gruyère
15ml (1 tbsp) dry white wine

In a small saucepan cook the carrot in the margarine or butter for 3 to 4 minutes. Stir in the flour, a dash each of white pepper and salt, and the tarragon. Add the milk, stirring constantly. Cook and stir till thickened and bubbly. To finish, add the Gruyère and white wine and continue cooking until the cheese melts.

Fish Pie

To serve 4 you will need:
225g (1 cup) rice
salt and pepper
juice of 1 lemon
white fish
30g (2 tbsp) butter
30 to 40g (2-3 tbsp) plain flour
2.5g (½ tsp) dry mustard powder
180ml (¾ cup) of skimmed milk

Cook the rice, seasoned with a little pepper and salt. Spread the cooked rice over the base of a flat baking dish or large pie plate. Sprinkle with the juice of one lemon.

Place the fish in an oven proof dish, sprinkle with lemon juice, salt and pepper, cover and bake for about 15 – 20 minutes (depending on the type of fish).

When fish flakes easily with a fork, drain the juices off and reserve. Lay the fish on top of the rice.

Make the sauce: melt the butter in a pan. Add the flour and mustard powder. Mix to a paste off the heat, and then add the juice from the cooked fish (mixing with a whisk or fork) and the milk. Return to low heat and cook until thickened.
Pour the sauce over the rice and the fish. Top with fresh breadcrumbs, chopped parsley and some grated cheese. Bake in the oven or under a grill until the top is brown.

Cooper's Sweet Fried Catfish

Badajoz was behind them. The rain had finally stopped, and as Cooper lay on the riverbank, the first bright sun of summer was warming him through. He had no duties, and there was half a bottle of brandy in the pocket of his discarded green jacket, wadded up under his head. Best of all, the very pretty maid from the tavern was stroking his forehead. Cooper was getting ideas…
What a time for that blasted cat-fish to finally take the bait! And it was huge - would he have any energy left after he'd landed it?!
Still, at least there'd be something very good for supper.

To serve 4 you will need:
4 catfish fillets, 4 – 6 ounces each
227g (1 cup) packaged sweet cornbread mix *or* 227g (1 cup) of mix, listed below
120ml (¹/₂ cup) oil for frying

Sweet cornbread mix - makes 500g (2 cups):
115g (¹/₂ cup) cornmeal or coarse milled dry polenta
170g (³/₄ cup) flour
170g (³/₄ cup) sugar
10g (2 tsp) baking powder
Mix well; store extra for future use.

Rinse and drain catfish fillets, but do not pat them dry.

Place cornbread mix in a large, resealable plastic zip bag. Add catfish fillets one at a time, shaking well to coat them evenly with the cornbread mix.

Heat the oil in a frying pan over medium heat. Cook fillets, turning them over only once, 4-7 minutes each side. Until you get a little experience with frying fish in this manner, it may be tempting to turn the fillets more often. Resist the urge! The cornbread mix won't stay on them if you fuss with them too much.

You will have to adjust the cooking time depending on how thick your fillets are. It's okay to use a spatula or fork to gently lift up a corner of a fillet to see if it is browning well or not.

Catfish is done when it flakes easily with a fork.

This is a perfect recipe for camping trips. Buy the largest box of sweet cornbread mix you can find and dedicate it to fish-frying. Store the mix in the plastic bags you intend use for coating your fish fillets – it travels well in a backpack in this manner and it helps simplify campsite cleanup.

When armies marched during the Peninsular War, it wasn't just the soldiers who moved through the countryside. Thousands of women—camp followers, prostitutes, and soldiers' wives—also traveled with the armies. Many wives of common soldiers had little choice; they received no pension, so for some the only choice was to accompany their husbands, or the workhouse. Not that the army encouraged marriage among its ranks—soldiers who wished to wed had to get permission from their superior officers, but only six men out of every one hundred who applied were allowed to marry.

Santiago Seafood Pasta

Sharpe and his riflemen had their first success at Santiago de Compostela, when they enabled the Spanish partisan leader, Blas Vivar, to raise the banner of Santiago in the Cathedral there (Sharpe's Rifles).

Before this, Harper and the other Riflemen had not regarded Sharpe as a 'proper officer'; afterwards, their loyalty to him was unshakeable.

It's doubtful that they would have had time to call in at a restaurant for this seafood feast, but they would have enjoyed it immensely had the French not been trying to kill them at the time!

To serve 2 you will need:

500g (2 cups) ready to eat mixed seafood
(mussels, squid rings, prawns)
1 onion
2 large cloves of garlic
400g (14 oz) tinned chopped tomatoes
100g (3 1/2 oz) sliced mushrooms
250ml (1 cup) white wine
(or more if you wish)
salt & white pepper to taste
400g (14oz) spaghetti (dried)
drop of olive oil
bunch of parsley

Chop the onion and garlic; sauté gently but do not allow them to brown. Add the wine and bring to the boil. As soon as it boils, add the seafood, mushrooms and tomatoes. Add salt and white pepper to taste. Simmer for about 8 minutes until the sauce is reduced by half. Check the taste half way through cooking and adjust seasoning if necessary.

At the same time, boil some water in a saucepan. Add the olive oil and some salt to the water. When water is boiling, add the spaghetti and cook on a rolling boil, following the manufacturer's instructions.

When the spaghetti is cooked, drain and put into serving bowls. Put the seafood mixture on top. Garnish with 4 green lip mussels in half shell, a twist of lemon and flat leaf parsley; serve with garlic bread.

If you avoid dairy products because you are lactose intolerant or vegan, try eating calcium rich foods like chinese cabbage (bok choy), kale, and broccoli – or adding calcium fortified fruit juices, tofu, and cereals to your diet.

Prawns Pycroft

To serve 4-6 you will need:
40-50 large prawns
30ml (2 tbsp) olive oil
42g (3 tbsp) unsalted butter
4 medium cloves garlic, minced
30ml (2 tbsp) fresh lemon juice
28g (2 tbsp) minced fresh parsley leaves
salt and ground black pepper

Sean Bean wasn't the only one to receive tinned pies while away from home. Lucky soldiers in the Peninsular wars might also receive care packages. William Surtees, an officer in the 95th, was the recipient of an unusual care package in late 1813. The large package from home contained

". . . two immense pies, weighing nearly a hundred-weight each, and packed in tin cases. They were composed of every kind of game and the best description of fowls, such as turkeys, &c., with the bonese taken out, and the meat baked till it became like brawn when cut in slices.
They were most excellent."

Peel and de-vein the prawns. Heat a 12-inch skillet over high heat until hot; 2 to 3 minutes. Add 15ml (1 tbsp) oil and swirl to coat the bottom of the pan. Add half the prawns and cook until just opaque, about 1 minute; transfer to a medium bowl. Return pan to heat and repeat process with remaining oil and prawns.

Return empty skillet to medium-low heat; melt 14g (1 tbsp) butter. Add garlic and cook, stirring constantly, until fragrant, about 30 seconds. Off heat, add the lemon juice. Whisk in the remaining butter; add the parsley, and season to taste with salt and pepper. Return prawns and accumulated juices to skillet. Toss to combine; serve immediately.

Serve prawns with plenty of chewy bread to soak up extra juices.

CHICKEN

Chickens had such a hard war. All over Portugal and Spain, they were falling off their perches, accidentally strangling themselves, losing their feathers and finding their way on to skewers over camp fires. The rules against looting were clear – but many officers, including Sharpe, were prepared to look the other way as long as a leg or a breast found its way on to their supper menu.

Sharpe got himself into considerable trouble for defending one of his most useless soldiers from provosts' justice in *Sharpe's Gold*. But every Company needed a whinging, light-fingered, ungrateful, work-shy private – and Batten was Sharpe's Company's prime specimen. They could be proud of him!
So, Private Batten – these are for you!

Chosen Men Chicken

I'm the world's laziest cook and this is absolutely the easiest way to fix chicken; plus it tastes great! The oven preheats while the butter is melting.

You will need:
60 to 115g (¼ to ½) cup butter
or margarine
115g (½ cup) flour
9g (2 tsp) paprika
2g (½ tsp) salt
1g (¼ tsp) pepper
chicken – *I use boneless breasts*

Preheat oven to 220°C/ Gas Mark 7/425°F

Put the butter or margarine in a roasting pan and place in the oven to melt; adjust the amount depending on how much chicken you're preparing — for 2 to 3 chicken breasts, 60g (¼ cup) is good.

While butter is melting, combine flour, paprika, and pepper in a large zip bag (baggie); salt the chicken and toss it into the bag to coat. When butter/margarine is melted, put the chicken in the pan and pop it into the oven.

Bake for 30 minutes, and then turn the chicken pieces. Bake for an additional 15 minutes, or until done.

Chinese Five Spice Chicken

To serve 4-8 you will need:
9g (2 tsp) salt
4.5g (1 tsp) sugar
1g ($^1/_4$ tsp) Chinese five-spice powder
30ml (2 tbsp) soy sauce
5ml (1 tsp) sesame oil
30ml (2 tbsp) Shaoxin wine or sherry or other cooking wine of your choice
1.8kg (4 lbs) chicken pieces

Preheat oven to 200°C/ Gas Mark 6/400°F

Mix together the first 6 ingredients. Add the chicken to the marinade, and marinate for at least a couple hours, I usually let them sit in the refrigerator overnight. Bake for 45 minutes or until done. The chicken pieces can also be grilled or broiled.

Ayre's Creamy Baked Chicken Breasts

Now you know what Provost Lt. Ayres did with all the chickens he collected from the men that he caught stealing.

To serve 4 you will need:
8 chicken breast halves, skinned and boned
8-10cm (4 inch) slices Gruyère
415g (10 $^3/_4$ oz) can cream of mushroom soup, undiluted
60ml ($^1/_4$ cup) dry white wine (or water)
230g (1 cup) herb-seasoned stuffing mix
60g ($^1/_4$ cup) butter, melted

Preheat oven to 180°C/ Gas Mark 4/350°F

Arrange chicken in a lightly greased 33x23x5cm (13x9x2 inch) baking dish. Top with cheese slices. Combine soup and wine; stir well. Spoon evenly over chicken; sprinkle with stuffing mix. Drizzle butter over crumbs; bake for 45 to 55 minutes.

Captain Leroy's Kentucky Hot Brown Dish

To serve 4 you will need:
240ml (1 cup) milk
14g (1 tbsp) butter
14g (1 tbsp) flour
57g ($^1/_4$ cup) grated Parmesan cheese
salt and pepper
57g ($^1/_4$ cup) American cheese
4 slices toast
4 slices turkey (or chicken), cooked
4 slices ham, cooked
8 strips bacon, fried crisp

Melt butter and blend in flour. Heat milk and whisk into paste. Bring to a boil over medium-high heat, stirring constantly. Salt and pepper to taste; blend in cheese.

Place a piece of turkey and a piece of ham on a piece of toast; cover with 60g ($^1/_4$ cup) sauce. Top with 2 strips cooked bacon and sprinkle with a tablespoon of Parmesan cheese. Repeat for remaining sandwiches.

Place under the grill until cheese melts and becomes golden brown.

Farmhouse Coq Au Vin

How do you keep a professional soldier home from the wars? Keep him well-fed, of course! Not even Richard Sharpe could resist Lucille's chicken in wine – can you?

To serve 4 you will need:
1 whole fresh chicken – or enough chicken pieces to equal a whole chicken
375ml (¹/₂ bottle) red wine – a wine you would drink for every day occasions; not too strong
2 large or 4 medium onions
170 to 225g (³/₄ to 1 cup) mushrooms, whole or thick sliced; any variety
115 g (¹/₄ pound) bacon, coarsely chopped
4 cloves garlic
Bouquet garni (or 4 bay leaves)
240ml (1 cup) chicken stock (optional)
butter
flour

In addition to calcium and vitamin D, there are other vitamins and minerals that can help improve bone density.
Magnesium and Potassium: The best sources for these minerals are in dark green vegetables like spinach, kale and romaine lettuce; other sources include tomatoes, bananas, and oranges.
Vitamin K: Look for this important bone-building vitamin in broccoli, cauliflower, Brussels sprouts, spinach, soy products, strawberries and liver. Cooking these foods with a little fat or oil will help absorption.
Vitamin C: Add oranges, grapefruit, lemons, cantaloupe, strawberries, peppers, broccoli, asparagus, cauliflower, tomatoes and potatoes to your daily diet to help make sure you get enough of this vitamin.

Cut the onions into small pieces and sauté in butter over moderate heat. Do not allow to burn. When cooked, transfer to a heavy-bottomed cooking pot. Using the same frying pan, cook the bacon, again ensuring that it does not burn. When it is done, add it to the cooking pot.

If using a whole chicken, cut it into approximately 10 pieces. Lightly flour the pieces and fry them in butter until golden brown. When they are cooked, put the pieces in the cooking pot.

Finely chop the garlic and add to the pot. Add the mushrooms, wine and chicken stock (if you don't have chicken stock, add a little more wine). Add salt and pepper to taste. Simmer for 45 minutes or until chicken pieces are very tender.

Serve with rice or potatoes.

This is the most basic version of this recipe. For flavour and variety, try adding any combination of the following to the pot:

A handful of small shallots or pearl onions
Peeled and quartered carrots
Cleaned and coarsely chopped celery
Fresh chopped thyme, to taste

Rifleman Lemon Chicken

Variant: Marching Camp Chicken

Ridiculously quick and easy for a meal in your billet.

To serve 4 you will need:
4 skinless, boneless chicken breasts
juice and zest of 2 lemons
5g (1 tsp) black peppercorns – some roughly crushed, some left whole.
crushed garlic (optional)

When a Rifleman reached for his weapon, it was a Baker rifle. In 1800 the British Board of Ordnance selected the Baker rifle, made by Ezekiel Baker from Whitechapel, as their weapon of choice. It was the first British produced rifle to gain acceptance by the British military—the few rifles that had previously been issued to soldiers were imported from Germany. The new rifle was 45 inches long, weighed almost nine pounds, and was fitted for a bayonet—a necessary addition for a soldier in this period. A convenience of the weapon was that the cleaning equipment needed to maintain the Baker rifle, and keep it ready for firing, was stored in the butt of the rifle.

Preheat oven to 200°C/Gas Mark 6/400°F
Rinse and place chicken in a shallow dish. Rub the zest and peppercorns into the meat. Pour the juice over it. Turn the breasts a few times to make sure every part gets coated. Cover dish closely with foil.
Bake for about 20 minutes. Discard the foil and spoon the juice over the meat. Replace in the oven for about 10 minutes. Check by inserting a fork to see if the juices run clear – if so – that's it. Great served with soufflé baked potato.

Variation:
(Barbecue to us modern softies)
First, of course, you will need to loot some chickens from a deserted village and not let the provosts catch you! Oh – and get Perkins to pluck and clean them…

Chicken pieces with the skin left on
Juice and zest of 2 lemons
Black peppercorns
6ml (2Tbsp) olive oil
Crushed garlic (optional)

Let the meat marinate in the other ingredients for an hour. Cook over camp fire until juices run clear. Alternatively, cook on the barbecue.

PORK

It is indeed strange how so many Franco-Iberian pigs seemed to lose the will to live when in close proximity to the British Army of the Peninsula. The army had strict instructions that they were not to loot or commandeer food. Provosts enforced the rules rigidly and looters could be hanged. But pigs died just the same.

Captain Fredrickson of the 60th Rifles was particularly lethal. The poor animals just appeared to lie down, put their trotters in the air and exsanguinate whenever his scarred face appeared. Perhaps he'd been brought up in a thrifty household and taught not to waste food, because the good Captain always felt obliged to consume the chops and other choice cuts, whilst his men were generous enough to help him out. If his good friend, Sharpe, was close by, then he was willing to help too – especially if the chops had a slice of kidney included.

These pork recipes are thus dedicated to Captain William Fredrickson.

Peachy Pork Tenderloin

To serve 4-6 you will need:
237ml (1 cup) peach preserves
30g (2 tbsp) brown sugar
5g (1 tsp) pumpkin pie spice
5ml (1 tsp) vanilla essence
907g (2 lb) pork tenderloin

Grill tenderloin over medium heat about 30 minutes or until desired 'doneness'. Meanwhile, combine peach preserves, brown sugar, pumpkin pie spice, and vanilla. During the last five minutes of grilling time, brush the tenderloin with one third of the peach mixture.

Heat the remaining peach mixture in the microwave until bubbly; serve over tenderloin slices.

Captain William Frederickson's Franco-Iberian Pork

Because of his special fondness for pigs!
This recipe has two different cooking methods; choose the one you prefer.
Captain Sharpe and his Chosen Men would have cooked the pork on a skewer over an open fire and turned it by hand.
You may prefer to use a rotisserie on a grill!

To serve 8-10 you will need:
1.25kg (3 lb) boneless pork loin
Marinade:
150ml (2/3 cup) dry sherry
150ml (2/3 cup) low sodium Soy Sauce
(1 3/4 cups) low sodium chicken stock
Add to this and stir until sugar is dissolved:
454g (2 cups) dark brown sugar
Add:
45g (3 tbsp) minced garlic

The Baker was reported to be more effective at long range than a Brown Bess, the standard British musket, but was not generally expected to be accurate much beyond 200 yards. Experienced riflemen, however, were often able to hit targets at a considerable distance—during the retreat to Corunna, Rifleman Thomas Plunkett of the 95th Rifles famously shot French General Colbert at what was judged to be a substantial range. Another concern about the rifle was that, because of the undersized lead balls they fired, one took longer to load than a musket; nevertheless, proficient riflemen learned to perform the task in twenty seconds, allowing them to fire at three shots per minute.

With the skin side of the pork loin facing you, cut numerous deep slits on the top and sides, about 5mm (1/4 inch) apart. Place your Marinade in a deep bowl and place pork loin skin side down in the Marinade. Cover and refrigerate for 10 to 14 hours. When you are ready to cook, remove the pork and, discarding the marinade, choose the cooking method you would like to use:

Method 1:

Place the pork loin on the rotisserie/skewers of your grill after the grill is heated to 200°C/400°F (moderately hot). Cook for 55 to 65 minutes until pork is done, but be careful not to over cook. Let the pork sit for 10 minutes before slicing. If you like your meat to have a charred look on the outside, start the grill at 260°C/500°F for the first 10 to 12 minutes, BUT you must lower the heat or the pork will over cook.

Method 2:

Place the pork loin in a roasting pan with 75ml (1/3 cup) water and bake at 190°C/375°F for 30 minutes. Check to see if you need to add more water (the water helps keep the meat from sticking to the pan and burning). Bake for another 20 to 25 minutes. Check to see if it is cooked to your liking; again, do not overcook. Pork is sufficiently cooked when it has reached an internal temperature of 71°C/160°F (a meat thermometer is helpful). Remove from oven and let sit 10 minutes before slicing.

Honey Barbecue Glazed Pork Roast

This is a slow cooker recipe.

To serve 6 you will need:

1.25kg (3 lb) boneless pork shoulder roast
118 ml ($^1/_2$ cup) barbecue sauce
59ml ($^1/_4$ cup) honey
45ml (3 tbsp) balsamic vinegar (preferred) or substitute any other type vinegar
5g (1 tsp) seasoned salt
150ml ($^2/_3$ cup) barbecue sauce
57g ($^1/_4$ cup) plain flour

If pork roast comes in netting or is tied, remove netting or strings and then cut away the visible fat from the meat. Place the roast in a 3.5L (4 qt) slow cooker. In small bowl, mix half of the barbecue sauce with the honey, vinegar, and seasoned salt; pour the mixture over the pork.

Cover; cook on low heat setting for 8-10 hours. Remove pork from cooker; slice and place on serving platter. Cover to keep warm.

In small bowl, mix the remaining barbecue sauce and the flour; gradually stir into juices in the cooker. Increase heat setting to high. Cover; cook about 15 minutes, stirring occasionally, until thickened. Serve sauce over pork.

Teresa's Ham in Wine Sauce

Although Teresa's domestic talents are rarely seen in the Sharpe books, any well brought up Spanish lady would have them. We know she could sew well, as she made a Rifleman doll for young Antonia. She and Sharpe had some time together in Salamanca after the battle there, so perhaps this is when she impressed her husband enough to reassure him that he would not starve when peace came . . .

To serve 4 you will need:

1 slice smoked or cooked ham, at least 2.5cm (1 inch) thick
30g (2 tbsp) butter
15g (1 tbsp) sugar
237ml (1 cup) red wine, suitable for drinking (Burgundy or Zinfandel)
15g (1 tbsp) cornflour
59ml ($^1/_4$ cup) cold water
227g (1 cup) seedless green grapes, cut in half

Melt the butter in a skillet; then sprinkle in the sugar. Brown ham on both sides. Remove ham. Add wine and bring to a boil, stirring. Combine cornflour and water and add to the wine mixture. Cook, stirring, until the sauce is thick and boiling.

Reduce the heat, add ham slice, cover and simmer 10 to 12 minutes longer. Add the sliced grapes and cook 5 minutes longer. Remove the ham, cut it into 4 pieces and serve sauce over it.

BEEF & OTHER MAINS

Wellington's Army marched on basic rations of beef, bread and rum. Cattle were herded with the army – or if this was not possible, then the meat was salted and stored in large barrels. The only way to make this edible was to boil it in large, unwieldy Flanders cauldrons, which each regiment was supposed to transport. The result was probably disgusting and no doubt the men added anything they could to the stew to make it more palatable.

We suggest that you forgo authenticity in this section, and use beef of a superior quality!

Cornish Pasty

Pastry rolled out like a plate,
Piled with turmut, tates and mate,
Doubled up, and baked like fate,
That's a Cornish pasty.
- old Cornish Rhyme

To serve 2 you will need:
Pastry:
1kg (4 cups) plain flour
500g (16oz) vegetable fat (or an even mixture of vegetable fat and butter)
cold water
pinch of salt
Sift the flour with the salt, cut or rub in the vegetable fat and mix to a pliable consistency with some water; cover with a dish cloth and leave it to rest for 30 minutes. Meanwhile, prepare the filling.

Filling:
500g (1lb) steak, cut in 1.2 cm ($^1/_2$ inch) cubes or 500g (1lb) minced beef
5 or 6 large potatoes, peeled and thin sliced
2 turnips or swedes, thin sliced
2 medium onions, peeled and chopped
salt and pepper

Preheat oven to 200°C/Gas Mark 6/400°F

Prepare all ingredients. Divide the dough into quarters and roll each piece into a round about 5mm ($^1/_4$ inch) thick. Lay potato slices thinly onto the centre of each round, overlapping slightly; repeat with the turnip slices. Finish by spreading the beef evenly over the vegetables; top with the chopped onion. Season with salt and pepper.

Dampen the edges of each round with water and bring the edges together in the centre, making a neat parcel. Make sure the pastry is well sealed; if holes appear in the dough, patch them with a little extra pastry.

Place the pasties on a greased baking sheet and make a small slit in the top of each to allow steam to escape. Brush tops with a little milk, if desired.

Bake at 200°C for 30 minutes, and then reduce the heat to 190°C/Gas Mark 5 /375°F and cook for 30 minutes more.

A Proper Roasted Beef

Preheat oven to 170°C or 190°C/Gas Mark 3 or 5/325° or 375°F

Start with the best quality roasting joint you can afford; sirloin, rump or topside are best. Larger joints make better roasts. Dust the meat with a little flour and season with mustard powder, salt, and pepper. Pour a bit of oil in the bottom of a heavy roasting pan. Thick slice the onion; place the slices into the bottom of the pan and top with the crushed garlic cloves. Put the joint on top of the onions.

Roast the meat, allowing 20 minutes for every 500g weight. Add an additional 15 to 20 minutes to reach your desired level of "doneness." You may want to turn the meat once during the cook time. It is far better to use a probe thermometer that you can leave in the roast rather than repeatedly poking the meat to test for doneness, as you lose juices every time your skewer it. Remember that the meat will continue to cook for a bit after you remove it from the oven.

Cover the roast with foil and allow it to rest on a plate for at least 20 minutes before you carve the meat. This is very important, as the resting time will allow the meat fibres to relax and reabsorb the juices.

You're going to need:
a good quality roasting joint of beef
dry powdered mustard
a large onion
3 garlic cloves, slightly crushed
salt and pepper
a bit of flour
a little olive or grape seed oil

Serve with roasted potatoes and your choice of fresh cooked tender crisp vegetables. Peas, carrots and beans are traditional. Most important – don't forget the Yorkshire Pudding!

Yorkshire Pudding

You're going to need:
100g (4oz) plain flour
pinch of salt
1 egg, beaten
300ml (1 cup) milk
25g (1oz) dripping, lard or butter

After you remove the roasted beef from the oven, turn the temperature up to 200°C/Gas Mark 6/400°F.

Sift flour and salt into a mixing bowl. Make a well in the centre and pour in the egg and half the milk. Beat the mixture with a wooden spoon, gradually drawing the flour into the liquid from the sides. When all the flour is incorporated into the liquid and a thick batter is formed, gradually beat in the remaining milk until the batter is smooth and of a pouring consistency.

Put the fat into a Yorkshire Pudding tin (or bun tray) and heat until bubbling in a hot oven. You may make one large pudding or small individual ones. Pour the mixture into the tin (bun tray compartments) and put back into the oven (20 minutes for individual puddings, 40 minutes for a large one), until well risen and golden brown. Remove from the oven and serve immediately.

"Ther't meyt hung dahn afore t'fire to rooast
Ther's t'puddin' on t'brandree afore it to tooast
Potatoes top o't hob, they'll be don enif sooin
But Ah thin tha can weive a few more bobbins bi nooin"
John Bramley, a weaver living near Leeds
Early 19th century

Sharpe's Slow Cooked Spaghetti Sauce

Although the British army of the early 19th century would not have been as familiar with pasta, it would not have been a total mystery. A sauce like this could have been eaten with other types of food in any case, and they were accustomed to both rice and lentils, as many soldiers, like Sharpe and Wellington himself, had served in India.

To serve 6-8 you will need:
500g (1lb) minced beef
500g (1lb) minced sausage
1 chopped green pepper
1 large chopped onion
4 garlic cloves, minced
1.2L (42 oz) tinned diced tomatoes
890ml (30oz) tomato sauce
350ml (12oz) tomato paste
30g (2 tbsp) sugar
30g (2 tbsp) dried Italian seasoning
15g (1 tbsp) dried basil
10g (2 tsp) dried marjoram
5g (1 tsp) salt
2.5g (1/2 tsp) pepper
cooked spaghetti or pasta of choice

In a large frying pan, cook beef and sausage until no longer pink – drain and transfer to a 4.7L (5 qt) slow cooker. Stir in green pepper, onion, garlic, diced tomato, sauce, paste, sugar, herbs and spices. Mix well. Cover and cook on low for 8 hours. Serve over pasta.

Even if pasta was an uncommon delight, the plains of Spain were rich with potential food sources for hungry British soldiers during the Peninsular Wars, as young Ensign Harry Smith of the 2nd Battalion 95th Rifles discovered: Upon these plains thousands of oxen and horses are grazing; they are so thick that were an individual ever entangled amongst them he would be lost as in a wood. These animals are, however, all the property of individuals, and not wild as supposed, and each horse and ox is branded. . . . The country abounds in all sorts of wild fowl and innumerable wild dogs, which nature must have provided to eat the carcases of the slaughtered cattle, many of which are killed merely for their hides, a few of the prime pieces alone being made use of for food. The marrow is usually also taken and rendered into bladders, with which they cook everything, using it, in short, as we use butter, which makes their dishes very palatable.

Written in Glasgow, 1824 – H. G. SMITH

Cottage Stew

To serve 3-4 you will need:
750g (1 2/3 lb) beef, suitable for casserole cooking
30ml (2 tbsp) flour
30ml (2 tbsp) butter
30ml (2 tbsp) vegetable oil
240ml (1 cup) beef stock
2.5ml (1/2 tsp) salt
pepper
2.5ml (1/2 tsp) dried thyme
2.5ml (1/2 tsp) dried marjoram
5ml (1 tsp) prepared mustard
30ml (2 tbsp) fresh lemon juice
45ml (2 tbsp) chopped parsley.

Cut meat into cubes.
Brown meat in butter and oil.

Combine meat with all the other ingredients except the parsley and lemon juice, and place in a slow cooker. Cook on LOW for 6 to 8 hours.

Stir in lemon juice and parsley just before serving.

Sharpe Shooter's Poacher's Stew

Any type of game can be used and pieces of chicken can be added to feed more mouths. I doubt if venison was very easily obtainable for Wellington's troops but pigeons, hares and rabbits and perhaps the odd road-kill pheasant would have been welcome additions to the pot (there must have been quite a few birds knocked flying by speeding carriages!)

To serve 8-10 you will need:

A variety of game and chicken, if using, cut into 8 - 10 portions
Salt and freshly ground black pepper
2 tablespoons of light olive oil
175g (6 oz) streaky bacon without the rind, chopped
4 large carrots, peeled and sliced into chunks
2 large onions, sliced
2 cloves of garlic, thinly sliced
2 tablespoons plain flour
300ml (1/2 pint) port, red wine or dry cider
300ml (1/2 pint) beef stock or water
2 bay leaves and freshly chopped parsley

Preheat oven 160°C/
Gas Mark 3/325°F

Dry the pieces of meat and season with salt and pepper. In the heated oil, fry the meat with the bacon until brown. Put into an oven-proof casserole or cast iron stockpot or even a slow cooker. Fry the onions and carrots in the same fat till lightly browned, add the garlic and fry for about 1 minute. Add the flour and mix in well. Then add the port (or whatever alcohol being used), stock, bay leaves and more salt and pepper. Bring to the boil and pour over the meat. Cover the casserole tightly and cook for about 1 1/2 hours, until tender - or suspend the stockpot over the campfire and have a few jugs of beer while it cooks. To serve, skim the surplus fat from the surface and sprinkle with parsley.

Dick Vaughan's Sausage Pie

It seems that Sharpe (using the name Vaughan) and Harper enjoyed wandering through the English countryside while looking for their 'lost' Battalion. The urgency of saving the South Essex from extinction could be temporarily forgotten as a friendly farmer's wife provided them with a hearty supper of sausage pie after a day of hedging. Plenty of good English ale would add to their happiness too!

To serve 6-8 you will need:

2 packets ready made puff pastry
500g (1lb) mild Italian or other spicy sausage meat
1 small onion, chopped
250g (1/2lb) Mozzarella cheese, diced or grated
125g (1/4 lb) Munster Cheese (or Edam), diced
2 Eggs
15g (1 tbsp) parsley
1.2g (1/4 tsp) pepper

Fry sausage with chopped onion and drain. In a greased 33 x 23 x 5 cm (13 x 9 x 2 inch) pan, roll out 1 packet of puff pastry. In a large bowl, combine: sausage, diced cheese, one egg, parsley and pepper. Toss and mix well. Place mixture on top of puff pastry in pan. Top with remaining packet of pastry and seal edges. Brush the top with one beaten egg yolk.

Bake 40 minutes. Cool and cut into desired shape and size. May be cut into smaller pieces for an appetiser.

Ramona's Baked Lamb Shanks

An easy meal that comes out succulent and tasty with a minimum of effort.

To serve 4 you will need:

4 lamb shanks
4 onions
4 carrots
salt and pepper
fresh or dried rosemary (optional)
oil for foil

The women who accompanied Wellington's army into the Peninsula, both wives – of which there were few – and camp followers – of which there were many more – performed many of the day-to-day tasks in the camps; washing and mending clothes, foraging for food, and cooking meals. Tools and utensils were virtually non-existent, and Patrick's good wife, Ramona, might well have used the same metal cauldron to make his porridge and wash his shirts!

Preheat oven 150°C/Gas Mark 2/300°F

Take four pieces of aluminium foil (cooking foil), each large enough to loosely wrap one of the shanks, and oil them lightly to stop sticking.

Put one piece of meat in the middle of each piece of foil and add one cut onion, one cut carrot, seasoning and rosemary if desired. Wrap loosely and place in a heavy oven dish. Repeat with the other three shanks.

Put in the oven for a minimum of two hours, but can be left longer – they just get juicier!

Sharpe's Rifles' Rabbit Pie

To serve 4 you will need:

1 rabbit, jointed, floured and browned
1 large onion, cut into chunks and browned
2 large carrots, cut into chunks
1 stick of celery, cut into 5cm (2 inch) chunks
1 bay leaf
6 black peppercorns
750ml (3 cups) chicken stock, vegetable stock, or water
salt
oil for browning
1 package ready-made puff pastry
English mustard
120ml (1/2 cup) double cream
flour and butter for thickening

Put browned rabbit, onion, vegetables, bay leaf and peppercorns into an oven-proof dish. Add salt to taste and pour over the stock or water. Cover with a lid or foil and bake for about 1 1/2 hours or until the rabbit is very tender. Cool and remove the flesh from the bones. Strain the liquid off and use to make a béchamel sauce with the flour and butter. Add the cream and 5 to 10ml (1 to 2 tsp) of mustard (more if you like it hot!!). Put rabbit and sauce into a pie dish and cover with the puff pastry. Make a hole in the top to vent the steam and brush with beaten egg or milk. Bake in a hot oven for about 20 minutes until golden brown.

Welsh Lamb Stew

Sharpe could well have enjoyed this after the battle of Fuentes del Onoro, (Sharpe's Battle) when Gog and Magog may have celebrated by cooking up a taste of home. Where they got the lamb from, I wouldn't care to think, but let's hope the provosts were looking the other way…

To serve 4-6 you will need:

680g (1½ lb) stewing lamb, diced
1 onion
2 or 3 leeks (use another onion if you can't get leeks)
113g (4oz) red lentils
113g (4oz) black lentils
57g (2oz) pearl barley (or dried split peas)
5ml (1 tsp) dried thyme
tin of chopped tomatoes
570ml (20oz) meat stock (stock cube is fine)
2 cloves of garlic (optional)
pepper and salt for seasoning.
2 turnips, cubed
3 potatoes, cut into chunks.
3 carrots, cut into chunks.

Put all the ingredients except the potatoes and carrots into a large pan or flame proof casserole dish and bring to the boil, stirring occasionally. Reduce to a simmer. Cover.

Either continue on the hob, stirring now and then and checking that the liquid isn't boiling away, or transfer to a slow, preheated oven (165-180°C/ Gas Mark 3-4/325-350°F).

You may need to add extra liquid — make sure it is very hot before you add it. After about 2 hours add the potatoes and carrots, and cook for another hour. Serve with any green vegetables and crusty bread.

Speed things up by using a pressure cooker — you'll need to cook at full pressure for about 10-12 minutes, then depressurise, add the potatoes and carrots. Bring back up to pressure and give it another 5 minutes.

Cheat by using frozen stew packs instead of fresh vegetables, but you'll still need the onions in the ingredient list.

Weight-bearing exercise promotes bone health, so after you've enjoyed your meal take some exercise for dessert! Good exercises include running, skipping, aerobics, tennis, weight training and brisk walking.

Colonel McCandless's Lentils with Rice

This recipe pays tribute to that rare breed – an army vegetarian. Colonel Hector McCandless played a vital part in young Richard Sharpe's rise from sergeant to the dizzy heights of the Officers' Mess. Without the colonel's encouragement and his influence with other senior officers, Sharpe would not have been raised to the officer class, no matter how many of the enemy he had fought off to save the life of Sir Arthur Wellesley.

To serve 4 you will need:
1 small onion, finely chopped
30-60ml (2-4 tbsp) extra virgin olive oil
125g (1/2 cup) lentils
375g (1 1/2 cups) long-grain rice
750ml (3 cups) of water
5g (1 tsp) salt
pepper

Wash and drain lentils; put in a 2L (2qt) saucepan with 3 cups (750ml) water. Bring to a boil, then turn down the heat to low, cover and cook for 20 minutes. Drain the lentils, reserving 2 cups (470ml) of the lentil cooking water; add more water to make 2 cups (470ml) if necessary. Set aside. Rinse and dry the saucepan, add the oil and slowly sauté the onions until golden. Add rice to the onions and stir so the grains are coated with the flavoured oil. Add the lentils and the reserved cooking water, season with salt and pepper and stir well. Bring to a boil. Turn heat to lowest, cover the pot with lid and cook for another 20 minutes. Do not open the lid during this period. Fluff the rice with a fork and serve.

Chosen Men Brown Rice & Lentil Stew

This recipe is cheap, tasty and can easily be produced in mass quantities. Simply increase measurements as appropriate to feed a company, regiment, battalion or army.

To serve 4-6 you will need:
170g (3/4 cup) brown rice
113g (1/2 cup) dried lentils, rinsed
113g (1/2 cup) chopped onions
113g (1/2 cup) sliced celery
113g (1/2 cup) sliced carrots
57g (1/4 cup) fresh parsley, snipped
5g (1 tsp) Italian seasoning
1 garlic clove, minced
1 bay leaf
590ml (2 1/2 cups) vegetable stock
400g (14 1/2 oz) tinned, whole tomatoes, undrained, chopped
15ml (1 tbsp) cider vinegar

Combine all ingredients and 500ml (2 cups) water in a large saucepan; bring to a boil.

Reduce heat and simmer, uncovered, stirring occasionally, for 1 hour, or until rice is tender.

Remove and discard bay leaf.

Ducos' Vegetable Cassoulet

To serve 4 you will need:
30-45ml (2-3 tbsp) olive oil
1 large. onion, chopped
3-4 cloves garlic, chopped
3-4 carrots, chopped
2-3 parsnips, chopped
425g (15oz) tinned cannelini beans,
drained and rinsed
1 block extra-firm tofu, cubed
vegetable stock, about 500ml (2 cups)
white wine
Herbes de Provence
salt & pepper

Preheat oven to 180°C/Gas Mark 4/350°F

In skillet, sauté the onion in a little olive oil. Add garlic when the onion is almost translucent and sauté for a further two minutes. Add carrots and parsnips, stir. Add spices, a good shot of white wine, stir again, lower heat and cover. Stirring occasionally, cook until the stubborn root veggies soften up (maybe 15 minutes). If it starts getting too dry, just add more wine.

Turn the vegetable mixture into a baking dish with a good cover. Add cubed tofu and beans. Gently stir until combined. Pour in vegetable stock until mixture is just covered. Add white wine to taste. Sprinkle more herbs and some salt and pepper over the top. Bake, covered, for 45 minutes. Uncover, raise the oven temperature to 200°C/Gas Mark 6/400°F and bake another 23-30 minutes or until liquids have reduced and the top is browned slightly.

Tip: *freeze & thaw the tofu in advance - the texture changes and it absorbs more of the juice & flavours.*

Harper's Indian Vegetable Korma

When Harper got tired of eating chicken and there was no beef to eat - or even a dead horse to be found - he could always resort to this mild vegetable dish.

To serve 4 you will need:
1 medium yellow onion, chopped
30g (2 tbsp) garlic, minced
1 medium jalapeno pepper, seeded and chopped
30g (2 tbsp) ginger/garlic paste

Heat ghee in a large fry pan; add the onion, garlic, pepper and ginger. Sauté until the onion is light brown.

Add and stir, mixing well:
250ml (1 cup) coconut milk
75g (5 tbsp) almond paste
15g (1 tbsp) cardamom powder
5g (1 tsp) mild curry powder
1.2g (1/4 tsp) cinnamon

Thoroughly blend the milk and almond paste; add the remaining ingredients and bring this to a boil, then reduce heat. After the heat is reduced;

Add:
500ml (2 cups) heavy cream
2 medium Charlotte, Yukon Gold or similar type potatoes, cut into bite-size pieces.

Simmer until the potatoes are tender and then add:
250g (1 cup) mini carrots (batons)
250g (1 cup) fresh green beans, cut in half
3 fresh firm (Italian) tomatoes, cut into large pieces
1/3 head fresh cauliflower, cut into pieces about 2.5cm (1 inch) wide
440g (15 1/2 oz) tinned chickpeas, rinsed and drained
500ml (2 cups) plain, unflavoured yogurt
salt to taste

Mix and cook until the vegetables are tender, 12 to 15 minutes; sprinkle with a few chopped fresh coriander leaves and serve with basmati rice.

Lucille's Cheese & Apple Flan

Suitable for vegetarians

To serve 4-8 you will need:

250g (8oz) plain flour
pinch of salt
125g (2oz) butter
cold water
2 cooking apples - cored and diced
(leave peel on if preferred)
500g (16oz) strong cheese (Farmhouse
Cheddar or similar) cut into small cubes
cinnamon (optional)

Maintain a healthy weight.
Being underweight increases your risk for
bone loss and fractures.

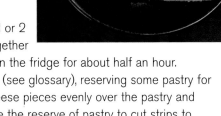

Oven temperature: 180°C/Gas Mark 4/350°F

Make the short pastry by rubbing the butter into the flour and salt until the mixture has the appearance of fine breadcrumbs.

Add the water a dessert spoon (10ml or 2 tsp) at a time and mix until bound together but not wet. Allow the dough to rest in the fridge for about half an hour. Roll out thinly and line a swiss roll tin (see glossary), reserving some pastry for decoration. Spread the apple and cheese pieces evenly over the pastry and sprinkle with cinnamon if desired. Use the reserve of pastry to cut strips to decorate.

Cook in the oven for about 20 minutes, or until the cheese has melted and the pastry is golden brown. Serve hot or cold as a main meal or part of a buffet.

Spinakopita (Spinach Pie)

This is a modern twist to my Grandmother's recipe.

To serve 8-10 you will need:

566g (20oz) fresh spinach, chopped
340g (³/4 lb) feta cheese, crumbled
680g (24oz) small curd cottage cheese
3 large eggs
1 large onion
2.5g (¹/2 tsp) salt
10g (2 tsp) pepper
500g (1 lb) filo (phyllo) dough
113g (¹/4 lb) butter or margarine, melted
125ml (¹/2 cup) vegetable oil
Note: Make sure the spinach, feta, and cottage cheese have as little excess liquid as possible.

Preheat oven to 180°C/Gas Mark 4/350°F

Combine first seven ingredients in a large bowl and mix thoroughly. Combine melted butter with oil in a separate bowl. With a pastry brush, coat a 33 x 23 x 5 cm (13 x 9 x 2 inch) pan with the butter and oil mixture. Line the pan with the phyllo dough, brushing each sheet with the oil and butter mixture, making sure to overlap the sheets and overhang the edge of the pan by 2.5cm (1 inch). Reserve 10 sheets of filo for the top. Pour the spinach filling into the pan. Layer the top with the remaining filo, brushing each sheet with the oil and butter mixture. Fold the overlapping filo over to seal. Pour a small amount of the remaining oil and butter mixture around edges of the pan to keep moist. Score the top into pre-cut slices. Bake for 45-60 minutes.

BREAD

Bread was one of the basics the army was supposed to provide for its soldiers. In winter semi-permanent camps it was usually possible to produce enough bread, even if the flour used was sometimes gritty. When the army was moving, things became tricky, with long supply lines, inadequate roads and limited supplies in the local countryside.

Twice-baked bread was one answer. Its dried-out texture was fine with the stews that were the usual main meals. Army biscuit was a last resort, and it was as hard as iron unless it was soaked well before anyone tried to eat it. Maybe that's what happened to Dan Hagman's teeth!

The soldiers would have thought themselves in heaven if they'd had access to the types of bread in this chapter. This is for Major-General Nairn, in tribute to the valiant efforts he and the newly promoted Major Sharpe made with a toasting fork before he sent Richard on yet another dangerous mission. (*Sharpe's Enemy*)

Baking Powder Biscuits

To make 2 dozen you will need:
280g (2 cups) plain flour
3.3g (1/2 tsp) salt
15g (1 tbsp) baking powder
60g (4 tbsp) vegetable fat or lard
180 to 240ml (3/4 to 1 cup) milk

Though most officers' wives remained at home, some chose to follow their husbands across Europe, suffering the same dangers and privations as their husbands. Juana Maria de Los Dolores de León sought protection from the British following the siege of Badajoz. A few days later she married Sir Henry (Harry) George Wakelyn Smith of the 95th Rifles. He was 24, and she was 14. Despite the speed of their courtship, they remained devoted to each other and Juana remained with her husband through the campaign, engaging in a remarkable series of adventures recounted by her husband in his memoirs.

Preheat oven to 190°C/Gas Mark 5/375°F

Sift together the flour, salt, and baking powder. With a pastry blender or two knives, work in the vegetable fat until the mixture resembles crumbs. Slowly add enough milk to make a stiff dough.

Turn dough out onto a surface coated with flour and knead it a few times; do not overwork the dough. Roll it out with a floured rolling pin or pat it out by hand to about 1.2cm (1/2 inch) thickness.

Cut into rounds. I use a jelly glass dipped in flour to cut them, but there are biscuit cutters made for this purpose.

Place on a greased biscuit sheet and bake for about 15 to 20 minutes, or until they are a nice golden brown. (It is possible to bake these at either a higher or lower oven temperature if you already have your main dish baking in the oven. Just be sure to watch that they don't get too dark.)

Yield for this recipe depends on the diameter of the biscuit cutter you're using. With a jelly glass I usually end up with close to 2 dozen biscuits.

Basic Battlefield Bread & Buns

You're going to need:

14g (¹/₂ oz) of Rapid Rise yeast (two packets)
480ml (2 cups) lukewarm water
100g (¹/₂ cup) sugar
13g (2 tsp) salt
910g (6¹/₂ cups) plain flour
113g (¹/₂ cup) margarine or butter flavour vegetable fat
3 eggs

On the 25th of August 1813, the officers of the 95th Rifles celebrated the 10th anniversary of their regiment. The fact that they were in earshot of the French bothered them not at all, and 73 officers sat down to a celebratory meal in a crude hut made from the tree branches. As no table or chairs were available, they dug trenches to dangle their legs in.

Preheat oven to 200°C/ Gas Mark 6/400°F

Dissolve the yeast in the water. Add sugar, salt, and half of the flour; mix well. Add eggs and vegetable fat, beat again and stir in remaining flour. Dough should form a soft ball. Turn out onto a lightly floured board and knead vigorously for 8 to 10 minutes.

Cover with a cloth and allow the dough to rise in a warm place until doubled in size. Punch down the dough and shape into the desired form (buns or bread). Cover and allow the dough to rise again until nearly doubled.

Baking time will vary, depending on what form you chose.

Beer Bread

This bread could have almost been a practical proposition for Sharpe's men, as its no fuss approach would have lent itself to their culinary skills. However, there would have been one slight, but fatal flaw - the beer. No, not how they got it – they probably had their ways – but how to save any of it for mixing in with the flour…

To make 1 loaf you will need:

420g (3 cups) of self-raising flour
113g (¹/₂ cup) sugar
355ml (12 oz) ale or other, fuller-bodied beer
113g (¹/₂ cup) butter

Heat oven to 180°C/ Gas Mark 4/350°F

Mix flour, sugar, and ale. Pour batter into lightly greased loaf pan and bake for 45 minutes. Remove from the oven, melt the butter and pour it over the top of the bread. Return to the oven and bake 10 more minutes.

Cheese Bread

To make 1 loaf you will need:
280g (2 cups) self-raising flour
8.4g (1¼ tsp) salt
3.3g (½ tsp) dry mustard
pinch cayenne pepper
2 eggs, beaten
180ml (¾ cup) milk
60ml (4 tbsp) oil or melted butter
340 + 57g (1½ + ¼ cups)
grated tasty cheese

Preheat oven to 200°C/
Gas Mark 6 /400°F

Sift dry ingredients into a bowl. Combine eggs, milk and oil (or butter) and add this mixture to the dry ingredients; mix well. Add 340g (1½ cups) of the cheese and fold through mixture. Place in a well-greased and base-lined loaf tin and sprinkle with the remaining grated cheese. Bake for 35-40 minutes.

Serve hot or cold, with butter.

S. A. Bread

An extra special recipe just for this book!

To make one loaf about 750g (a little over a pound and half) you will need:

The overnight soaker:
150g whole wheat flour (1 cup)
150g water (¾ cup)
¼ teaspoon yeast
Mix above with a spoon in a big bowl, cover and let sit overnight.

The final dough:
300g plain flour (2½ cups)
150g water (¾cup)
6g salt (1 teaspoon)

Add the final dough ingredients to the big bowl of overnight soaker. Stir well with a wooden spoon or a dough whisk. Let sit for 30 minutes. Knead until smooth as a baby's bottom. Cover with a piece of cling film, let rise until doubled. Turn dough out onto a floured board, knead a few times and form into a ball. Cover with a towel and let it sit and relax for 30 minutes.

Line a 7" plastic basket with a clean dish towel or napkin, sprinkle flour liberally all over. Sprinkle the top of the dough with flour. Use a skinny rolling pin or a dowel (about 1" to 1.5" diameter), press down the dough ball right at the centre, down to the board but do not sever it. Remove the pin and sprinkle flour into the crack. Crease the dough a second time with the dowel or pin, slightly widening and reinforcing the split. Sprinkle with more flour. Gently pick up the dough, turn it upside down, put in the prepared basket. Cover and let it proof until doubled.

Preheat oven to 425°F. Line a baking sheet with parchment paper. Carefully turn the dough onto the lined baking sheet, split side up. Spray dough with water, bake at 425°F for 20 minutes, Turn oven down to 375°F for another 25 minutes.

This shape is called fendu, a split bread. You can also just use your own favourite dough recipe, and shape it this way to make your own SA bread.

Harris's Famous Gooey Bread

You're going to need:
1 loaf sweet French bread
240ml (1 cup) mayonnaise
1 onion, finely chopped
75g (1/3 cup) Parmesan cheese, grated
325 to 450g (1 1/2 to 2 cups)
cheese, grated
(use Cheddar, Monterey Jack or similar
– or a blend of favourite cheeses)
5ml (1 tsp) Worcestershire sauce
(or Henderson's Relish)
5g (1 tsp) garlic powder or 2-4 fresh
garlic cloves, minced
paprika

Slice bread loaf lengthwise. Mix all of the ingredients, except paprika, and spread on both halves of the bread. Sprinkle paprika over the top. If you want to freeze for a later use, freeze it unwrapped (to avoid the topping sticking to the plastic wrap) until stiff and then wrap well until needed.

Bake at 200°C/Gas Mark 6/400°F for about 15 minutes or until cheese is melted and begins to brown.

Serve hot.

Sour Simmerson's Lemon Loaf

This light and lovely lemon loaf might even have improved the sour disposition of the obnoxious Sir Henry Simmerson.

To make 1 loaf you will need:
113g (1/2 cup) butter
227 + 57g (1 + 1/4 cup) caster sugar
(measure amounts separately)
5g (1 tsp) baking powder
2 eggs
340g (1 1/2 cups) plain flour
118ml (1/2 cup) milk
grated rind from 1/2 of a lemon
juice of 1 lemon

Preheat the oven to 190°C/Gas Mark 5/375°F.

Lightly grease (or spray with butter flavour non-stick cooking spray) a 454g (1lb) loaf tin. Line the base of the tin with waxed paper.

Cream the butter until light and fluffy. Add 227g (1 cup) sugar. Add the eggs one at a time, beating well after each addition. If you like, you can add a little flour to keep the consistency smooth during this step. Stir in lemon peel. Sift the flour and baking powder together and fold the dry ingredients and milk alternately into the creamed mixture.

Pour the batter into the prepared tin. Bake 45-55 minutes, until the top is well risen and a toothpick inserted in the middle of the cake comes out clean.

Let the cake stand for 10 minutes. While you're waiting, mix together the lemon juice and remaining sugar. Pour over the cake and allow it to finish cooling, then turn out on to a serving plate.

Sharpe's Rations

Feast and Famine in Regency England

Supplying the British Army of the Peninsula was very difficult, especially as the army moved into Spain, already ravaged by internal disputes and the depredations of the French provisioning officers. Perhaps fortunately, most of the infantrymen were accustomed to shortages of food, coming as they did from the most desperate groups in British society.

The differences between rich and poor in early 19th century Britain were much more sharply drawn than today. The labouring classes could afford only the cheapest kind of food, such as bread and oatmeal. Very little meat was consumed, even in the countryside, as the animals were far too valuable to be eaten by the poor. Even farmers needed to sell their cattle and sheep for rent money. Some of the cheapest cuts of pork and a little bacon was all that was available for the typical family.

The lower class of inhabitants live on meal of oats, and barley, and potatoes, and fish, with a small proportion of fleshmeat. Their breakfast is of meal pottage and milk; their dinner is potatoes, and either salt or fresh fish; sometimes beef or pork, as they can afford; and their supper either pottage, or potatoes and milk. What bread they use is made of barley meal, which is cheaper than oat meal, and is considered as more wholesome. The labourers have a small piece of ground for the growth of potatoes; and those who keep cows are obliged to cultivate some corn for their provender. ~B. Quayle, General View . . .

The Prince Regent, the future George IV, as lampooned by James Gillray, 1792

By contrast, the rich often ate gargantuan meals consisting of many courses, with huge quantities of meat. The firmly corseted Prince Regent and most of his brothers were testimony to the fact that this level of consumption had its effect on the figure. The greed of the royal family was a contributing factor in their unpopularity in the Regency period. Political cartoonists were grateful for the easy target this gave them though.

The Army reflected the same kind of gap between rich and poor. Officers and enlisted soldiers had very different treatment when it came to rations. Wellington was probably fairer to his soldiers than most commanders, knowing that half-starved men would not have the stamina for hard campaigns, long marches and exhausting battles. He worked hard to get the money for much needed supplies.

Wellington's soldiers were paid a shilling a day, out of which money was taken for their food and drink. The money was deducted even if the rations were only partially delivered, as in the early years of the campaign in Spain. Further sums of money were deducted for laundry, for lost equipment and for supporting the institutions which looked after wounded veterans. The men received little more than one third of that shilling when their pay was handed over.

The rations look somewhat less than healthy to us, consisting of bread, beef and rum, The beef was often in short supply, the bread often became the infamous 'ship's biscuit' or the 'twice-baked' variety. The rum usually got through!

Most officers could afford much better food, and the Officers' Mess was supplied with the pick of what was available. The rotund Wagon-Master General Runciman of *Sharpe's Battle*, no doubt made full use of the mess resources.

Sharpe's circumstances sometimes meant he had difficulty meeting his mess bills. But Sharpe had a long history of overcoming adversity and short rations – advantages Runciman had not experienced. These stemmed from Sharpe's childhood, when he had been abandoned to the mercies of the dreaded workhouse.

Richard Sharpe was brought up in a workhouse after the death of his mother. Workhouses were dreaded by the poor. They were run on the principle of making conditions uncomfortable to discourage people from using them unless desperate.

Pauper children were expected to work hard from a very young age; Sharpe still bore the scars of oakum picking on his hands as an adult. If he hadn't run away into a life of crime, he would almost certainly have been sold off to an employer as an 'orphan apprentice' to work in a factory or as a climbing boy chimney sweep. Most of these children didn't live to grow up.

In the reports following the reform of the poor law in the 1830s there were stories of the inmates of a Yorkshire workhouse being fed from a communal trough. There were deaths in a Hampshire workhouse when some of the half-starved inmates, given the job of crushing bones from a slaughterhouse for use as bone-meal fertiliser, sucked the bones to extract the rancid marrow. The most famous condemnation of workhouse conditions comes not from the newspapers of the period, but from Charles Dickens. 'Oliver Twist' was written in 1838/9, but conditions at the time of Sharpe's childhood, fifty years earlier, would have been very similar.

Boys have generally excellent appetites. Oliver Twist and his companions suffered the tortures of slow starvation for three months: at last they got so voracious and wild with hunger that one boy, who was tall for his age, hinted darkly to his companions, that unless he had another basin of gruel per diem, he was afraid that he might some night happen to eat the boy, who slept next to him, who happened to be a weakly youth of tender age. He had a wild hungry eye, and they implicitly believed him. A council was held; lots were cast who should walk up to the master after supper that evening, and ask for more; and it fell to Oliver Twist. ~ Charles Dickens, "Oliver Twist"

Young Richard Sharpe was no sweet-faced Oliver Twist, and had no 'lost' family in whose bosom he would eventually find comfort. Sharpe was a street-wise urchin with a potentially lethal ability to stand up for himself and for what he believed to be right.
He was also to get his revenge upon the sadistic Master of his childhood orphanage, but this had to wait until he was an officer and not always a gentleman!

Sharpe's first company, the 33rd Regiment of Foot, were nicknamed the Havercakes, after a traditional Yorkshire staple.

TO MAKE A HAVERCAKE

Take two pound of dryed flour after it has been searced fine, one pound of good sugar dried and searced, also a little beaten sinamon or some nottmegg greeted and steeped in rose water; so straine two eggs, whites and all, not beaten to it, as much unmelted butter as will work it to a paste: so mould it & roule it into longe rouses, and cutt of as much at a time as will make a cake, two ounces is enough for one cake: then roule it in a ball between your hands; so flat it on a little white paper cut for a cake, and with your hand beat it about as big as a cheese trancher and a little thicker than a past board: then prick them with a comb not too deep in squares like diamons and prick the cake in every diamond to the bottom; so take them in a oven not too hot: when they rise up white let them soake a little, then draw. If the sugar be dry enough you need not dry it but searce it: you must brake in your eggs after you have wroat in some of your butter into your flower: prick and mark them when they are cold: this quantity will make a dozen and tow or three, which is enough for my own at a time: take off the paper when they are cold. To take on campayne, bake one more tyme until quite dry when crumbled in hand.

Desserts

Desserts

It was probably a very rare event for the soldiers to have desserts. They would opt for a drink or two after their meals instead. In fact, they'd opt for that drink before, and during meals too! So in this case we will ask an army veteran of many years to introduce this section...

"I've nothing to say, sir!" **Obadiah Hakeswill, RIP** *(please!)*

Better than Sex Cake
That's the name...honest!!

To serve 16 you will need:
1 packet yellow cake mix or 1 packet Victoria sponge mix
1 whole egg
2 egg whites
30ml (2 tbsp) oil
326ml (1 1/3 cups) water
567g (20oz) tinned, crushed pineapple, packed in juice, slightly drained
113g (1/2 cup) sugar
473ml (2 cups) milk
small packet vanilla dessert mix
5ml (1 tsp) vanilla extract
3 large bananas, peeled and sliced
454g (16oz) sweetened frozen strawberries, thawed and drained
57g (1/4 cup) flaked coconut, lightly toasted
340g (12oz) non-dairy whipped topping
113g (1/2 cup) chopped pecans

Pre-heat oven to 180°C/ Gas Mark 4/350°F.

Coat a 33 x 23 x 5 cm (13 x 9 x 2 inch) pan with non-stick spray. In a mixing bowl, beat cake mix, egg, egg whites, oil, and water together on low speed for 1 minute, scraping bowl constantly, or beat 2 minutes with a large spoon or wire whisk. Pour into pan.

Bake cake for 29 to 34 minutes, until toothpick inserted into centre comes out clean and top springs back when touched in the centre. About 5 minutes before cake is done, combine pineapple and sugar in a small saucepan and boil gently for 5 minutes. Remove cake from oven and make holes in the top with a toothpick or fork. Pour cooked pineapple over hot cake. Set aside on wire rack to cool.

When cake is cool, pour milk into a medium bowl and add pudding mix. Beat with a wire whisk or electric mixer on low speed for 2 minutes. Stir in vanilla and spread over cake. Evenly place banana slices, then strawberries over the pudding, then sprinkle with coconut. Next spread the whipped topping over the coconut. Sprinkle with nuts. Store in the refrigerator.

Rifleman's Honey Cake

To serve 16 you will need:
450g (1 lb) self raising flour
240ml (1 cup) oil – sunflower or vegetable
5g (1 tsp) baking powder
5g (1 tsp) bicarbonate of soda
6g (1 heaped tsp) ginger
180ml (3/4 cup) clear honey
6ml (1 heaped tsp) mixed spice
240ml (1 cup) oil tepid water
3 medium eggs
flaked almonds

Heat oven to 170°C/Gas Mark 3/325°F

Weigh, measure and mix all the dried ingredients together. Slowly whisk the eggs together and add the honey, oil and water. Slowly add the dried ingredients to the liquid, beating all the time until the mixture is light in colour and bubbles rise to the top.

Mix all ingredients and divide the mixture between two small roaster size tins that have been lined with greaseproof paper. Sprinkle flaked almonds on top of cake and place in oven. Bake for about 25-30 minutes. One large size roaster takes about 30-35 minutes; it depends how hot your oven is!

Sharpie's Bizcocho

To serve 16 you will need:
Using the yoghurt pot as a measure:
1 pot of yoghurt (150g), lemon or plain
3 medium eggs
1 yoghurt pot of olive oil
2 yoghurt pots of caster sugar
3 yoghurt pots of self-raising flour

Note: You can use a larger size yoghurt pot as a measure but you might need to add another egg!

Heat the oven to 150°C/Gas Mark 2/350°F (fan assisted oven) or 175°C/Gas Mark 3/375°F (normal oven)

Mix all the ingredients together and beat until smooth.

Add grated zest of 1 lemon (optional - add a handful of raisins, some chopped apple or sprinkle with cinnamon). Pour into a lightly greased baking tin (approximately 26 x 36cm/10 x 15 inch). Bake for 40 minutes.

Prinny's Chocolate Cake

Sharpe's supper with the Prince Regent was a change from the mess tent – 28 courses, though most were lukewarm since the kitchen was a bit distant. We don't know precisely which dishes were served at the supper, but odds are the rather pudgy Prinny would have appreciated this cake.

To serve 16 you will need:
Preheat oven to 200°C/
Gas Mark 6/400°F

THE CAKE INGREDIENTS
Mix together in large bowl:
454g (2 cups) sugar
454g (2 cups) flour
2.5g (1/2 tsp) salt

Mix together in saucepan:
113g (1/2 cup) butter
118ml (1/2 cup) oil
237ml (1 cup) water
57g (4 tbsp) cocoa

Heat saucepan contents to boiling. Immediately pour over the dry ingredients in the bowl.

Add to the bowl:
2 eggs
118ml (1/2 cup) buttermilk
5g (1 tsp) baking soda
5ml (1 tsp) vanilla essence

Stir until smooth. Pour into an ungreased swiss roll tin and bake for 20 minutes.

THE ICING INGREDIENTS
While the cake is baking, prepare the icing:

113g (1/2 cup) butter
46g (3 tbsp) cocoa
89ml (3oz) milk

Place ingredients in a saucepan, mix well, and heat until boiling. Remove from heat and add:

454g (2 cups) icing sugar
5ml (1 tsp) vanilla
113g (1/2 cup) nuts (optional)

Mix well (add more milk if the icing is too stiff). Spread icing over hot cake as soon as it is removed from the oven.

Vitoria Celebration Cake

The South Essex not only distinguished themselves at the Battle of Vitoria (Sharpe's Honour), but they got back their 'executed' Major Sharpe - and the Major got the Marquesa de Casares el Grande. Naturally she showed her gratitude to him for freeing her and restoring some of her wealth − modesty prevents us from telling you how! She also had this special cake made for the double celebration of the victory and Sgt. Harper's marriage. The lemon in it makes it a bit lighter than the usual rich fruit cake − of course, it's best to use Spanish lemon to make it authentic!

To serve 12 you will need:

284g (10oz) plain flour
142g (5oz) self raising flour
9g (2 tsp) mixed spice
284g (10oz) butter
284g (10oz) caster sugar
510g (18oz) dried fruit (any mixture of sultanas, raisins and currants)
85g (3oz) glacé cherries
113g (4oz) Brazil nuts
grated zest of one large lemon
4 large eggs, beaten
1.2ml (¼ tsp) almond essence
2.5ml (½ tsp) vanilla essence
30ml (2 tbsp) lemon marmalade
30 to 45ml (2 to 3 tbsp) milk

Preheat oven to 170°C/Gas Mark 3/325°F

The size of the cake tin is important − you need a 23cm (9 inch) round tin. If you want to make a smaller diameter cake, you must reduce the quantities.

Sift together the flours and spice into a bowl. Add the lemon peel. Put the dried fruit into another bowl. Add the halved Brazil nuts. Wash and halve the cherries and add to the bowl. Mix all the fruits together.

In a large mixing bowl, cream the fat and sugar until light and fluffy. Beat in the eggs and essences a little at a time. Little by little fold in some of the flour, then some of the fruit, alternating until it is all used. Stir the marmalade with a fork to break it up. Stir this into the mixture and add enough milk to make a dropping consistency.

Line the baking tin with a double thickness of greaseproof paper/baking parchment. Cut out two more rounds to fit on top of the cake, and tie a band of brown paper around the outside of the tin. Put the mixture into the tin and cover with the double thickness of greaseproof paper.

Bake for 1 hour and then reduce the heat to 150°C/Gas Mark 2/300°F and cook for about another 2 hours. Test with a metal skewer about ½ hour before the cooking time is up. When the skewer comes out clean, the cake is cooked. Allow the cake to cool in the tin for about ½ hour, and then remove to a wire rack to finish cooling; remove the paper very carefully. Wrap in foil to store. This is a good cake to decorate with marzipan and icing for Christmas or other celebrations.

Wellington's War Cake

Unfortunately, every generation has some variation on this recipe; this one is from the Second World War when rationing was imposed in Canada and ingredients were scarce. When I was growing up my great-grandmother still made it regularly, sometimes jazzing it up with icing or serving it dusted with fruit sugar.

Heat oven to 180°C/Gas Mark 4/350°F

To serve 12 you will need:

Boil together until the vegetable fat melts and the sugar dissolves:

454g (2 cups) raisins
473ml (2 cups) water
454g (2 cups) brown sugar
32g (3 tbsp) vegetable fat

When cooked, let stand until cool and then add:

5g (1 tsp) cinnamon
2.5g (1/2 tsp) nutmeg
680g (3 cups) flour
5g (1 tsp) soda
2.5g (1/2 tsp) salt

Turn into a greased cake pan and bake at 350° for about 1 hour.

Hagman's Best Vinegar Pie

To serve 8 you will need:
342g (1 1/2 cup) sugar
14g (1 tbsp) polenta
27ml (1 1/2 tbsp) vinegar
(or lemon juice if you prefer)
5ml (1 tsp) vanilla essence
113g (1/2 cup) butter, melted
1 prepared pie shell

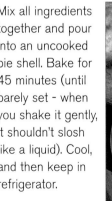

Preheat oven to 180°C/Gas Mark 4/350°F

Mix all ingredients together and pour into an uncooked pie shell. Bake for 45 minutes (until barely set - when you shake it gently, it shouldn't slosh like a liquid). Cool, and then keep in refrigerator.

Vitamin D helps improve calcium absorption! The sun is your best source; if you can't get enough, consider supplementing your diet with 10mg/400iu every day.

Loyalist Black Bottom Pie

Like Sharpe, Captain Leroy never quite fit into the stratified world of British army's officers' ranks – but as a former denizen of the American South, he could have offered up a few delicacies to atone for his colonial origins. This extravagant pie, with layers of chocolate custard, rum chiffon, and whipped cream, would have undoubtedly met the approval of even the most high minded of Wellington's officers.

Tools:

A bain-marie; 2 large, 1 medium, and 1 small mixing bowls; whisk, metal spoon, rubber spatula ; hand, stand, or rotary mixer; willpower, to avoid over "sampling"

To serve 16 you will need:

14g (1 tbsp) unflavoured gelatin
75ml ($^1/_3$ cup) water
14 + 9g ($^1/_2$ + $^1/_4$) cup sugar
21g (1$^1/_2$ tbsp) cornflour
1.2g ($^1/_4$ tsp) salt
354ml (1$^1/_2$ cups) whole milk – do not use reduced fat milk
3 large eggs, separated (save both yolks and whites)
57g (2 oz) unsweetened chocolate, finely chopped or melted
5 + 2.5ml (1 + $^1/_2$ tsp) vanilla essence
59 to 118ml ($^1/_4$ to $^1/_2$ cup) good quality rum
1 23cm deep dish pie case, baked

In a small bowl, sprinkle the gelatin over the water and set aside to soften. In the upper pan of the bain marie, mix 113g ($^1/_2$ cup) of the sugar, the cornflour, and the salt. Add the milk in a steady stream, whisking constantly to avoid lumps. Lightly beat the egg yolks and then add them to the mixture; whisk until evenly blended. Cook the mixture over boiling water, whisking almost constantly, until it boils. Reduce the heat and continue to cook until the custard thickens.

Remove from the heat and pour about 177ml ($^3/_4$ cup) of the hot custard over the chocolate in a small bowl; add 2.5ml ($^1/_2$ tsp) vanilla. Stir until the chocolate melts, then spread the chocolate mixture into the bottom of the pie shell and set aside. Add the gelatin to the remaining custard and blend. Pour the mixture into a large bowl; add remaining vanilla and the rum. Place in the refrigerator, whisking occasionally, until it is cool but NOT set. Shortly before the custard is cooled, whip the egg whites in a large bowl until soft peaks form. Add the remaining $^1/_4$ cup sugar and continue beating until they form stiff peaks. Pour the cooled custard over the egg whites; FOLD gently until blended. Spread the mixture in the pie tin, cover loosely with cling film and refrigerate until firm (several hours).

226g (1 cup) double cream
22g (1-$^1/_2$) tbsp sugar
Vanilla and almond essences
Grated unsweetened chocolate

Prepare the topping; whip the cream with the sugar until stiff, adding the essences to taste about half way through. Spread over the pie, covering it completely. Sprinkle the grated chocolate over the top. Keep refrigerated until serving.

Prince of Orange Trifle

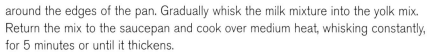

To serve 8-10 you will need:

Custard:

4 egg yolks
113g (1/2 cup) granulated sugar
75g (1/3 cup) cornflour
710ml (3 cups) whole milk (do not use reduced fat milk)
28g (2 tbsp) grated orange peel
89ml (3 tbsp) frozen orange juice concentrate

Sponge Cake:

4 eggs, separated
170g (3/4 cup) granulated sugar
5ml (1 tsp) vanilla essence
113g (1/2 cup) plain flour
pinch of salt

Assembly:

237ml (1 cup) orange marmalade
237ml (1 cup) whipping cream
75ml (1/3 cup) orange liqueur (Grand Marnier or Cointreau will also work, or use orange juice concentrate instead)
850g (30oz) tinned mandarin orange slices, drained
icing sugar

For custard: In a medium bowl, whisk together the egg yolks, sugar, cornflour and 118ml (1/2 cup) milk; set aside.

In a heavy saucepan, heat the remaining milk with the orange peel over medium-high heat for 5 minutes or until bubbles form around the edges of the pan. Gradually whisk the milk mixture into the yolk mix. Return the mix to the saucepan and cook over medium heat, whisking constantly, for 5 minutes or until it thickens.

Remove the pan from heat and stir in the orange juice. Transfer the custard to a bowl and place waxed paper directly onto the custard surface. Place the custard bowl into the refrigerator and completely cool, approximately 4 hours. (The custard can be refrigerated for up to 2 days.)

For sponge cake: Line a 27 x 39cm (15 x 10 inch) swiss roll tin with waxed paper, and heat oven to 190C/Gas Mark 5/375F.

In a deep bowl, beat egg yolks with 113g (1/2 cup) sugar for 5 minutes, or until it is thick and pale. Blend in the vanilla extract. In a separate bowl, beat the egg whites until soft peaks are formed. Slowly beat in the remaining 59g (1/4 cup) sugar until glossy, stiff peaks form. In a third bowl, combine the flour with the salt.

Alternately, fold egg white and flour mixture into the yolk mix, starting and ending with the egg whites, in 3 additions. Spread evenly into the prepared pan and bake for 14 minutes or until the top springs back to the touch.

Dust a clean dish towel with icing sugar. Run a knife around the edge of the cake to loosen and upend onto the towel. Carefully peel off the wax paper. Beginning at the long side, tightly roll up the cake in the towel and let cool. Unroll cake and spread with marmalade; reroll tightly without the towel. [The cake can be stored for up to 3 days ahead or frozen up to a week.] Cut into 1.2cm (1/2 inch) thick slices.

TO ASSEMBLE: Whip the cream to stiff peaks. Whisk the custard to loosen and fold in half of the whipped cream. Reserve the remaining whipped cream. Line the bottom of a 10-cup trifle bowl (or deep wide glass bowl) with one third of the cake slices. Brush with half of the orange liqueur. Line the sides of the bowl with another third of the cake slices. Spoon a third of the custard mix into the bowl. Cover with a third of the mandarin orange pieces. Top with the remaining cake slices and brush with remaining liqueur. Spoon another third of the custard mix over the cake slices, and arrange another third of the mandarins on top and at the edges of the bowl to show through the glass. Cover with the remaining custard. Spread the reserved whipping cream on top and decorate with the remaining mandarin pieces. (This trifle can be covered and refrigerated for up to 1 day.)

Tiramisu Talavera

To serve 8-10 you will need:
2 packets ladyfingers (boudoir biscuits)
250g Mascarpone cheese
600ml (20 oz) coffee, allowed to cool
400ml (14 fl oz) Marsala wine
(or sweet sherry – but note that
the taste is *not* the same!)
3 eggs, separated
chocolate for grating
a large, rectangular dish.

Make up the coffee, fairly strong, and allow it to cool.
While the coffee cools, add the Mascarpone to the egg yolks and beat until smooth. In a clean bowl, beat the egg whites to a stiff peak. Fold the egg white into the combined yolks and Mascarpone until well blended.

Add the Marsala to the cooled coffee. Dip the ladyfingers two at a time into the coffee and Marsala, taking care not to leave them too long or they will disintegrate.

Line the bottom of a 22cm (8 inch) square dish with the ladyfingers and spoon a thin layer of the cheese mixture over them. Repeat these two layers twice, making sure that the last layer of mixture is thick enough to cover completely the ladyfingers.

Grate chocolate over the entire surface and refrigerate covered with clingfilm overnight; it will become nicely firm. Serve alone or with pouring cream, fruit etc.

Maggie Joyce's Peach Crumble

Maggie was uncertain about taking in a young runaway from a foundling home, but she provided Richard Sharpe with a home and a bit of comfort. Though peaches were a luxury during this period, Maggie's connections would likely have allowed her to acquire enough to make this delicious crumble for her streetwise lad.

To serve 4-6 you will need:
675g (1 1/2 lb) fresh peaches, sliced
150g (5oz) plain flour
75g (3oz) butter
75g (3oz) caster sugar
1.25ml (1/2 tsp) ground cinnamon

Preheat oven to 180°C/ Gas Mark 4/350°F

Grease a 1L (1 3/4 pint) pie dish. Place the peaches in the bottom of the pie dish. Using a fork, food processor or your hands, blend the butter (roughly cut), flour, sugar and cinnamon until the mixture resembles fine breadcrumbs. Distribute the mixture evenly over the peaches and press lightly into place.

Bake for 30-40 minutes until the crumble topping is golden brown.

Chocolate Chip Cookies

To make 2 dozen you will need:
227g (1 cup) butter flavoured vegetable fat
170g (3/4 cup) sugar
227g (1 cup) brown sugar (eg: Billington's Molasses Sugar)
2 eggs
7.5ml (1 1/2 tsp) vanilla extract
511g (2 1/4 cups) cake flour (you can substitute with self-raising flour - omit salt and baking powder)
5g (1 tsp) salt
7.5g (1 1/2 tsp) baking powder
454g (2 cups) chocolate chips

Heat oven to 190°C/Gas Mark 5/375°F

Mix shortening and sugars. Add eggs and vanilla. In a separate bowl, sift cake flour (or self-raising), salt and baking powder. Add flour mix to vegetable fat mix in 3 batches. Stir in chocolate chips. Chill batter about 10 minutes (just until firm). Grease a cookie tin and drop batter by spoonfuls onto the tin. Bake 13-15 minutes, until the edges are brown.

Note:
For tender cookies, use more brown sugar, less white sugar. For a chewier cookie, use darker brown sugar.

Earl Grey Tea Cookies

These cookies are very light, very delicate, and very addictive!

To make 6 dozen you will need:

5 + 20g (1 + 4 tsp) loose Earl Grey tea
(use a tea bag if there is no loose tea on
hand - just open the bag
and measure out)
177ml (3/4 cup) hot water
75g (1/3 cup) light brown sugar
75g (1/3 cup) cup granulated sugar
75 + 7.5g (1/3 cup + 1 1/2 tsp) unsalted
butter softened
1 egg
1.2ml (1/4 tsp) pure vanilla extract
170g (3/4 cup) plain flour
1.2g (1/4 tsp) salt

Preheat oven to
180°C/ Gas Mark
4/350°F

Combine 1 teaspoon
of loose tea with
boiling water and
steep; strain and
refrigerate the mix
until chilled. Blend
remaining tea and
brown sugar until it
becomes a fine
powder.

Mix the tea sugar,
granulated sugar and
1/3 cup butter and
beat until light. Add
vanilla, 3 tablespoons of the brewed tea and egg and beat until smooth. Gently
add in the salt and flour. Cover and let stand for 30 minutes.

Lightly grease 2 large baking trays. Drop slightly rounded 1/2 teaspoons of batter
onto the sheets. Spread the batter into 2-inch rounds. Bake the cookies until
golden and the edges begin to darken. Cool on the sheets for 1 minute, and then
carefully transfer them to a wire rack. (Cookies can be stored in an airtight bag
for 1 week or frozen for several months.)

*When Arthur Wellesley, later the first Duke of Wellington, promoted Richard Sharpe, he
ran counter to a tradition that not only favoured gentlemen as officers, but also those
gentlemen who could pay for the privilege. Until 1871, the accepted method of attaining
a commission was to purchase it – ranks up to, and including, Lieutenant Colonel could
be bought; the majority of British officers during the Peninsular Wars had purchased
their ranks.*

Jane Sharpe's Quick Cookies (Cheater Cookies)

It was the "Merry Widow", Molly, who encouraged Jane's social ambitions and her betrayal of Sharpe. It could be that the two met over one of Jane's genteel tea parties as she was trying to climb the social ladder. The name is somehow appropriate…. These cookies may have a lot to answer for!

To make 2 dozen you will need:
567g (20oz) Oreo, Hydrox, or other similar cream-filled biscuits
227g (8oz) soft creamed cheese
1kg (36oz) chocolate chips
10g (2 tsp) butter

Blend biscuits in a food processor until they are finely ground, and then add the creamed cheese a little at a time.
Continue blending until the mixture looks black again.

Roll the mixture into small balls about 2.5cm (1 inch) in diameter; place them on wax paper and refrigerate until firm. Melt the chocolate chips with the butter in a saucepan over medium heat. Dip the chilled cookies into the melted chocolate and refrigerate again till set.

Laura's Famous Oatmeal Cookies

To make 2 dozen you will need:
227g (1 cup) vegetable fat
227g (1 cup) brown sugar
227g (1 cup) white sugar
2 well-beaten eggs
5ml (1 tsp) vanilla essence
340g (1 1/2 cup) sifted plain flour
5g (1 tsp) salt
5g (1 tsp) baking soda
680g (3 cups) quick-cooking oats
340g (12 oz) butterscotch chips

Preheat oven to 180°C/ Gas Mark 4/350°F

Thoroughly cream the vegetable fat and sugars. Add eggs and vanilla, beat well. Add dry ingredients to creamed mixture and beat well. Stir in oats and chips. Drop by tablespoonfuls onto an ungreased baking sheet. Bake for 8-10 minutes. DO NOT OVERCOOK!

Sauce Belle Marquesa Helene

To serve 10 you will need:

Quantities are approximate:

125g (4.5oz) dark chocolate (preferably 70% cocoa or better)
700ml (1¼ pt) pear nectar (the really thick kind that has pulped pears in it)
50ml (2oz) Creme de Cacao (the brown variety)
50ml (2oz) vodka
(if you can't find the Creme de Cacao, use 100ml vodka instead)
10 ml (½ oz) groundnut oil or other more-or-less flavourless oil
- be aware of nut allergies!

Help yourself help your bones -
Quit smoking and only consume caffeine
and alcohol in moderation!

Melt the chocolate in a bain marie over medium heat. When it is melted, add the oil and stir in; turn the heat to high and ensure that the chocolate is fairly hot:

Warm 10ml of the pear nectar and add very slowly, folding it in as you go. Once added, stir for a minute or two to reheat the chocolate. Using the same technique, add 20ml more of the nectar and reheat again. Repeat with another 100ml.

By now, the mixture should be sufficiently emulsified to remain liquid, so add the rest of the nectar, still fairly slowly, stirring continuously. If the mixture starts to curdle (separate) turn the heat up and use a hand blender to re-emulsify it.

Once all the nectar has been added, turn off the heat & remove the mixture from the bain marie. Allow to cool for 10 minutes or so & then add the spirits. Stir for 5 minutes during which quite a bit of the alcohol will evaporate from the mixture. Adjust alcohol content to taste. Serve poured over pandoro, panettone, ice cream, pancakes . . .

Keeps in the fridge for up to two days and makes enough for approximately ten servings.

Sweet William's Cinnamon Apples

Spicy yet sweet inside, just like our Sweet William. These apples would be easy for Fredrickson to eat since they're cooked until soft.

To serve 6-8 you will need:
1.4kg (3 lbs) cooking apples, peeled, cored, and quartered
255g (9oz) cinnamon candy

Place apples and cinnamon candy in a pan over medium heat. Add a small amount of water, if desired, to help the candy melt more quickly. Stir occasionally until apples are translucent. Remove apples, chill.

Sharpe's Christmas Apples

Two days after Christmas, 1813, and the Rifle Officer and his Sergeant-Major were re-visiting the field where they had failed in their duty earlier in the week. The South Essex had postponed their Christmas dinner in order to do what they did best – confound the French. But there was no avoiding it this time – those bullocks had to be shot if the men were to get their roast beef feast.

A bullock looked at Sharpe with its sad, gentle eyes. Sharpe sighed, and handed his rifle to Harper. Harper knew he should not look into the bullock's eyes – but he couldn't resist. He handed back the rifle and produced a bottle of French brandy from his pocket.

'Harris and Cooper will do it, sir – if they get a spot of lubrication to help them along'

Yes – the most feared warriors in Wellington's army had been defeated. But they did buy a few sacks of apples from the farmer on whose land Sharpe's conquerors were grazing. And this gave the regiment the best dessert that they could ever remember.

To serve 4 you will need:

4 large apples
100g (3.5oz) of flaked almonds
30g (1oz) butter
20g (4 tsp) brown sugar
2.5g (1/2 tsp) cinnamon
148ml (10 tbsp) Calvados
or other apple brandy
or use apple juice for an alcohol free dish
125ml (8 tbsp) cream
4 scoops of pistachio ice cream

If you already suffer from osteoporosis, take extra care in your day-to-day activities to prevent falls. Things you can do to make your home safe include:

- *Keep your rooms bright and well lit*
- *Keep your floors clean and clear of any obstructions*
- *Make stairs safe by keeping them uncluttered*

Heat oven to 199-220°C/ Gas Mark 3-4/390-430°F

Peel the apples and carefully remove the cores. Cut off a 2.5cm (1 inch) slice from the top of each apple and carve a cavity about the size of a small ice cream scoop in the lower section. Place the slice back on top of each apple. Stick the apples on the outside with almond splinters (this gives them a bit of a hedgehog look).

Grease an oven safe casserole with 10g (0.3oz) of butter and add the apples; add the rest of the butter in slices, sugar, cinnamon and the calvados or apple juice. Place in the oven on moderate heat and bake until the apples are soft but stable, maybe 35 minutes depending on the apples used. Baste with the juices several times while baking.

Remove from oven and place the apples on individual serving dishes.
Heat the cream and add the juices from the pan of apples, stirring until mixture is hot.

Take off the top of each apple, put in a scoop of ice cream and replace top. Spoon the sauce into each plate and serve immediately.

Glossary

"England and America are two countries separated by a common language." ~ **George Bernard Shaw**
"What on EARTH is THAT?" ~ **a Sharpe Chef**

A

Agi-no-moto: Monosodium Glutamate; sometimes known as Chinese salt.

Almond Bark: dark, white or milk chocolate poured over whole almonds, cooled and broken into pieces.

Almond, Flaked: slivered or almond splinters

Angel Food Cake Tin: one or two piece fluted cake tin, with higher, straighter sides than a savarin, ring or bundt pan

Agar Agar: vegetarian gelatin substitute

Apples, Bramley: variety of cooking apple; very large, very tart. Compare to Granny Smith.

Apples, Gala: variety of eating apple; small, sweet and mild. Available in the UK and US.

Apples, Rome: variety of cooking apple; medium large, semi-tart. Compare to Monarch.

Aubergine: eggplant

B

Baggie: polythene bag

Baking Powder: sodium bicarbonate with acidifying agent; can be made by mixing two parts sodium bicarbonate to one part cream of tartar

Bain Marie: double boiler

Baking Soda: pure sodium bicarbonate; CAN NOT be substituted for baking powder in recipes

Beans, Garbanzo: chickpeas

Beans, Navy: haricot or white beans

Bicarbonate of Soda: baking soda

Broil: grill

Broiler: griller

Bundt Pan: one piece ring-shaped cake tin with rounded sides, often scalloped or otherwise decorated.

Bundt Pan, 12 cup: bundt pan, 12 hole

Butter, Cube: see butter, stick

Butter, Stick: = $^1/_4$ lb = $^1/_2$ cup = 8 tbsp

C

Canola Oil: canola is a trademarked cultivar of genetically engineered rapeseed variants from which rapeseed oil is obtained. Also known as "LEAR" oil (for Low Erucic Acid Rapeseed)

Catsup: ketchup

Cheese, American: processed/blended cheese, often in slices but also available in blocks

Cheese, Monterey Jack: unaged, mild semi-soft, melting cheese; also found as aged, hard, grating cheese.

Cheese, Munster: in the US, a mild cheese with a smooth, orange rind. French Munster is round and has a stronger flavour.

Cheese, Velveeta: pasteurised, processed, blend of orange cheeses, soft and creamy when melted.

Chickpeas: garbanzo beans

Chocolate Chips: chocolate crumbles

Chocolate Crumbles: chocolate chips

Cilantro Leaves: coriander leaves, also called Chinese or Mexican parsley

Coriander: seeds of the coriander plant (leaves are known as coriander leaves or cilantro).

Corn Syrup: processed sweetener made from corn, often modified with enzymes to increase the glucose content.

Cornmeal: polenta. Packaged dry.

Cornmeal, Enriched: cornmeal/polenta with added vitamins. Packaged dry.

Cornstarch: cornflour

Courgette: zucchini

Cracker, Butter Flavoured: cream cracker

Cracker, Cream: butter flavoured cracker

Cream, Single: half & half cream

Cream, Whipping/Double: heavy cream

Crème Fraiche: cream slightly fermented and thickened with lactic acid (light sour flavour)

Crescent Rolls: pre-packed puff pastry.

Crumb Crust: a pie case made by crushing graham crackers, Oreos or other sweet biscuits, combining with a binder such as butter and perhaps including sweeteners and/or spices. The mixture is then pressed into a pie tin and baked.

Crumb Topping: a loose, crumbled topping for pies, cobblers or other baked items. Made by combining sugar, butter, crushed biscuits/oatmeal/flour and spices and sprinkling over the top of the dish to form a "crust."

Currant: dried, black seedless grapes from the Corinth grape (hence its name).

D

Double Boiler: bain marie

Dutch Oven: a heavy, cast-iron pot with tight-fitting cover that can be used in the oven for stews or casseroles. Sometimes called a French Oven.

E

Eggplant: aubergine

Elbow Macaroni: see Pasta, Elbow

EVOO: Extra Virgin Olive Oil

F

Flour, Plain: white flour, medium protein content for general baking

Flour, Bread: white flour, highest protein content

Flour, Self Raising: white flour, medium protein, with an added leavening agent (i.e. baking powder)

Flour, Whole-Wheat: whole meal flour

French Oven: see Dutch Oven

G

Golden Syrup: thick, amber-colored form of inverted sugar syrup.

Grill: broil

Griller: broiler

Ground Meat: minced meat

Groundnut Oil: peanut oil

H

Hand Blender: stick or immersion blender

Half & Half Cream: Single cream

Hard-Cooked Eggs: hard-boiled eggs

Heavy Cream: Whipping/Double cream

Hydrox Cookies: round, dark chocolate biscuits sandwiched together with a white cream (similar to Oreo Cookies).

I

Immersion Blender: stick or hand blender

J

Jell-O: a brand of flavoured gelatin dessert. May be purchased pre-made or in powdered form.

Jelly Roll Pan: swiss roll tin

K

Karo Syrup: corn syrup. Three varieties are available: White (with added vanilla and high fructose corn syrup), Dark (with added refiners syrup and caramel colour/flavour to simulate molasses), and Pancake Syrup (with added maple flavouring).

Ketchup: catsup

Kielbasa: spicy pork sausage, substitute chorizo

Kosher Salt: coarse-grained salt without additives, traditionally used for removing blood when koshering meat.

L

Lime, Household: calcium hydroxide or calcium oxide, often called for as a crisping agent in pickling recipes. The two compounds can be used interchangeably as long as the package is clearly labeled hydrated, slaked, builder's, or household lime. *Neither compound should be used if the package is labeled agricultural, burnt, or quick lime.*

Liquid Smoke: A brand name for a smoke-flavoured food additive used to simulate the flavour of an open fire.

Lumpia Wrappers: sometimes called Shang-hai-style egg roll wrappers, these skins are used typically to prepare lumpia, savoury Filipino egg rolls. The wrappers are made from flour and water, or cornflour, eggs, and water.

M

Maggi: dark sauce similar to soy sauce (but without soy)

Minced Meat: ground meat

Molasses: black treacle

O

Oats, Quick-Cooking: rolled groats cut into pieces to speed cooking time

Oats, Rolled: steamed & flattened groats (not a substitute for Steel-cut oats)

Oats, Steel-cut: whole grain groats roughly cut into 2 or 3 pieces (do not substitute rolled or quick oats). Sometimes called Scottish or Irish oatmeal.

Onions, Spring or Green: scallions

Oreo Cookies: round, dark chocolate biscuits sandwiched together with a white cream (similar to Hydrox Cookies).

P

Pasta, Elbow: small tubes of dried pasta formed into a semi-circular shape similar to a bent elbow

Peanut Oil: groundnut oil

Pear Nectar: pear juice thickened with pureed fruit

Polenta: cornmeal

Polenta, Enriched: cornmeal/polenta with added vitamins

Pudding, Instant: "Pudding" in the US, refers to a chilled dessert with a mousse-like consistency – not a general term for the sweet course taken after a meal. Instant pudding is a packaged, dry mix that can be combined with milk and chilled. It does not require cooking.

Puff Pastry: crescent rolls

R

Raisin: dark brown, wrinkled, sweet, sun dried grapes, usually from seedless white or black grapes picked and dried on the stalks.

Raisin, Sultana: soft, sweet, juicy, amber-coloured, sundried grapes, usually from the Thompson seedless grape.

Red Hot Candies: cinnamon candies (i.e. Hot Tamales, Cinnamon Hearts, etc.)

Reese's Peanut Butter Cups: brand name for peanut butter-filled chocolate cups.

Rutabaga: Swede

S

Salmon, Sockeye: tinned red or pink salmon

Sausage, Andouille: spicy pork sausage, substitute chorizo.

Sausage, Kielbasa: spicy pork sausage, substitute chorizo.

Savarin Tin: a ring-shaped cake tin with rounded sides

Scallions: spring onions, green onions

Sesame Paste: Tahini

Shallots: small pink or brown skinned onions. Substitute scallions/spring or green onions if necessary.

Shortening: fat or oil in solid form. Vegetable fat, lard, margarine or butter. Substituting butter or margarine for vegetable fat or lard in baking will give slightly different results.

Sour Cream: strong version of créme fraiche

Stick Blender: hand or immersion blender

Sugar, Brown: unrefined/partially refined sugar or white sugar with molasses added (113g ($1/2$ cup) brown sugar=113g ($1/2$ cup) white sugar + 30ml (2 tbsp) molasses). May also substitute Muscavado Sugar.

Sugar, Caster: superfine sugar/berry sugar

Sugar, Icing: powdered sugar/confectioner's sugar

Sugar, Powdered: Icing sugar

Swede: Rutabaga

Swiss Roll Tin: jelly roll pan

T

Tahini: sesame paste

Treacle, Black: Molasses

Tube Pan: one or two piece ring shaped cake tin, sometimes called an angel food cake tin

V

Vanilla Essence: vanilla extract

Vegetarian Ground Beef: vegetarian meat alternative, i.e. texturised vegetable protein, Quorn (TM), soy

Z

Zatar, Za'atar: blended Middle Eastern spice including sesame seeds and salt as well as oregano, thyme, cumin or sumac.

Zucchini: courgette

REFERENCES

Adkin, Mark   *The Sharpe Companion: A Detailed Historical and Military Guide to Bernard Cornwell's Bestselling Series of Sharpe Novels.* London: HarperCollins Publishers, Ltd., 1998.

-*The Sharpe Companion: A Historical and Military Guide to Bernard Cornwell's Sharpe Novels, 1777-1808: the Early Years.* New York: Perennial, 2005.

Brears, Peter C. D.   *Traditional Food in Yorkshire.* Edinburgh: J. Donald Publishers, 1987.

Costello, Edward   *Rifleman Costello: The Adventures of a Soldier of the 95th (Rifles) in the Peninsular & Waterloo Campaigns of the Napoleonic Wars.* Eyewitness to war series. [UK]: Leonaur, 2005.

Dickens, Charles   *Oliver Twist.* London: Chapman and Hall, 1838.

Edden, Helen   *Traditional Recipes of Old England.* New York: Hippocrene Books, 1996.

Gillray, James   "A voluptuary under the horrors of digestion." London: H. Humphrey, 2 Jul 1792. Library of Congress, Prints & Photographs Division, [reproduction number, e.g., LC-USZ62-123456]

Hughes, Kristine   *Everyday Life in Regency and Victorian England: From 1811-1901.* Cincinnati, OH: Writer's Digest Books, 1998.

Kincaid, John   *Adventures in the Rifle Brigade by Captain John Kincaid of the 95th Regiment (later the Rifle Brigade).* First published in 1830; republished in 1997 by Leo Cooper (an imprint of Pen & Sword Books Ltd.)

Leach, Jonathan   *Rough Sketches of the Life of an Old Soldier.* Cambridge: Ken Trotman, 1986

Lees, Belinda & Theya Molleson   "Differences in proximal femur bone density over two centuries." *Lancet* 341, no 8846. 1993

Quayle, Basil   *General View of the Agriculture of the Isle of Man. With Observations on the Means of its Improvement.* London: C. MaCrae, 1794.

Raynor, Keith   "Riflemen of the 95th Regiment (Rifles) at Corunna 1808-1809" http://www.militaryheritage.com/riflemen.htm. Accessed 16 Jun 2007.

Smith, George W.   *The Autobiography of Lieutenant-General Sir Harry Smith, Baronet of Aliwal on the Sutlej, G.C.B.* Edited with the addition of some supplementary chapters, by George Charles Moore Smith. London: J. Murray, 1903.

Surtees, William   *Twenty-five Years in the Rifle Brigade.* London: Frederick Muller LTD, 1973.

Talley, Ryan Jason   "Over the Hills and Far Away …" *A Study of the 95th Rifles: Their Background, Discipline, Doctrine, and Combat Employment during the Defense of Portugal, 1810-1811.* Thesis (M.A.)—University of Richmond, 1998.

Urban, Mark   *Rifles: Six Years with Wellington's Legendary Sharpshooters: A Work of Narrative History Tracing the Story of the 95th Rifles.* London: Faber and Faber, 2003.